Rick,

With thanks for your contribution to our book and admiration for your accomplishments in public health.

Bill

Ardith

Copyright © 2017 C. William Keck and Ardith Keck

"Alone we can do so little; together we can do so much."[1]

Helen Keller

---

[1] Keller, Helen. Brainy Quotes. Available at: https://www.brainyquote.com/slideshow/authors/top_10_helen_keller_quotes.html

WORKING TOGETHER...
ON COLLABORATION

By C. William Keck, David Kettlewell & Ardith Keck

Why You Should Read This Book

As individuals, we can only accomplish so much . . . but together, we can do great things.

This sums up the principal focus of this book: how to collaborate effectively and work with others.

The steps to successful collaboration are explained in some detail, and to this is added the cumulative experience and I suppose we can say, wisdom, of many professionals well familiar with the dynamic of working with others.

The focus of this book is principally how organizations can work together, but it is equally valid for individuals working with other individuals.

So if you want to work effectively with others and with other organizations, this book is for you.

FOREWORD

Working Together . . . On Collaboration by C. William Keck and his coauthors, David Kettlewell and Ardith Keck, accomplishes two tasks. Its primary intent is to create a book to assist those who are interested in collaboration to create something that can and will benefit the health of communities. The second task is to create a unique kind of festschrift for Dr. C. William Keck, an outstanding figure in public health. They have expertly completed both tasks.

Dr. Keck has held major leadership positions in public health, including president of the American Public Health Association and The Council on Education for Public Health, which accredits schools and programs in public health. He has served since 1988 as the chair of the Public Health Foundation's Council on Linkages between Public Health Academia and Practice. For many years, he was simultaneously the director of health for the City of Akron Health Department and an academic leader at the Northeast Ohio Medical University.

Dr. Keck certainly knows collaboration. In the book, he presents generalizations about the importance of collaboration and some of the principles he has learned through the years from his personal experience. He also provides us with concrete examples of successful and unsuccessful collaborative efforts and the lessons he has taken away from those experiences.

His thoughtful comments are further developed by a series of colleagues who, in interviews, discuss their own notions of and experiences with collaboration. These interviews provide insights from a pantheon of individuals whose life and work have intersected with Dr. Keck's. These individuals represent important leaders in a number of areas, notably public health (as would be expected) but also those he has worked with in his efforts to acquaint the US health care system with the Cuban system of care.

All of them are Dr. Keck's close colleagues, and they frequently refer to Dr. Keck and his leadership, wisdom, mentorship, and thoughtfulness in working with others. These laudatory references make the book a bit of a well-deserved, thoughtful tribute to such a kind and generous human being.

The book concludes with some illustrative stories and reflections from Dr. Keck and his wife, Ardith, an important partner in his efforts through the years.

Our own research team has recently written about organizations and agencies in communities that established multi-sectoral collaborations to improve community health. The principles that Dr. Keck and his colleagues describe closely follow our research, both the extensive literature review that we did early on to set up the framework for our research and the results of the research effort themselves. In our study of a limited number of community collaboratives designed to improve community health, the same lessons that Dr. Keck describes were also key to the success of our study communities. We know that nearly 50% of collaborations fail, and Dr. Keck describes his own experience with failures to establish or maintain collaboratives.

In full disclosure, Dr. Keck and I have also worked together in a major collaboration, the production of the *Principles of Public Health Practice*, a labor of love for the two of us as coeditors. It illustrates many of the lessons and comments that Dr. Keck discusses. We have learned together how to create three editions of the book—with publisher changes, editor changes, authors who promised and didn't deliver a chapter on time, or a chapter that we wouldn't publish without major revisions. So I share many of the same lessons with him as well as the interviewees' admiration for Dr. Keck, whose primary mission in life is to improve the health of the public he serves.

Dr. Keck and his colleague, David Kettlewell, and wife Ardith have produced an excellent book that describes from Dr. Keck's and his wife's experience, along with those he has worked with over time, a series of principles and lessons learned from their experience of collaboration, primarily in public health. It contains object lessons that can help both the neophyte and those with experience working with others to create new health collaboratives. Anyone who takes on this difficult and often unsuccessful and unappreciated task will benefit by the knowledge that is shared in the book. If you are in the beginning of such an effort or considering doing a collaborative, the lessons he and his colleagues describe will hold you in good stead and will make this book a worthy addition to your library.

F. Douglas Scutchfield, MD
Bosomworth Professor of Health Services Research and PolicyColleges of Public Health and Medicine
University of Kentucky
Lexington, Kentucky

PREFACE

I began this book project as a reluctant participant. I had been fully retired for six years after working in public health for over four decades. The great bulk of that work time was spent simultaneously as a full-time public health practitioner and a part-time academician striving to excel in both areas while building stronger bridges between the two. It was a career that suited my interests and abilities, and I left it with a sense that I had managed it reasonably well with successes outweighing failures.

A few years ago some friends and colleagues suggested that I should help teach a younger generation by writing a book about my experiences, particularly those relating to collaborative ventures. Quite frankly, I didn't feel comfortable with the idea. After all, I know many others who have had effective careers, and writing about myself in that way just seemed too immodest. Despite growing pressure from a few to proceed, especially my friend David Kettlewell, I continued to demure. When David suggested that we might proceed with a book that would include my experiences, along with others whose collective experiences might allow us to tease out lessons learned about the ins and outs of collaboration, I began to feel much more positive about the idea. When I shared that idea with a number of friends and colleagues and received, for the most part, encouragement to proceed, my reluctance was replaced with some enthusiasm.

The book you hold in your hands is the result of the decision we made to push ahead. The "We" includes David, my wife, Ardith, and me. The three of us worked as a team on all aspects of creation of the book and had a fine time doing so.

Ardith has not only been active in many collaborative arrangements herself; she has also been my companion, confidant, advisor, supporter, and constructive critic since we met at age 15. And she has been an integral part of both my personal and professional life since then. The role she has played for me exemplifies what we believe is important for anyone seeking to become involved in complex collaborations, a trusted and "safe" confidant who can provide unbiased advice.

Some formal research has been done on understanding the components of successful collaborations. We reference that at the end of "On Collaboration," the first major section of the book.

Our intent, however, is to bring the elements described to life by sharing stories and insights not only from Ardith's and my experience but also from the experiences of others who have built—or tried to build—successful collaborations. The majority of our contributors come from the practice or academic worlds of public health, but a few from other disciplines are included as well. This is not a typical textbook with each paragraph heavily referenced—far from it. It is a compendium of stories from a wide range of personalities used to compile a guide that we hope will be useful to our readers. Collaboration can be a daunting prospect, and we hope you will be encouraged and energized—and perhaps even amused at times— by what follows.

C. William Keck, MD, MPH

ACKNOWLEDGEMENTS

The success of a book like this depends upon the good will of very busy people. Our colleagues who agreed to be interviewed about their views and experiences related to collaboration have our sincere thanks for their contributions. The time they devoted to interviewing and editing is appreciated.

No book is complete until it is well edited, and Gail Kerzner of The Savvy Red Pen did a superb job for us. Jim Vaughan of James Vaughan Photography designed our cover, and Mike Blanc of Artists Incorporated guided the book's layout.

Lois Arnold, James Boex, Pete Crossland, Diane Kraus, Sue Phillips, and Elaine Rasmussen are friends and colleagues who have our special thanks for reading and commenting on a draft of the manuscript.

TABLE OF CONTENTS

FOREWORD 9

PREFACE 13

ON COLLABORATION 21

INTERVIEWS

    Bill Keck 61

    Ron Bialek 77

    Ricardo Martinez 89

    Betty Bekemeier 109

    Paul Erwin 119

    Gail Reed 127

    Virginia Caine 139

    Chuck Vehlow 157

    Donna Petersen 167

    Caswell Evans 183

    Amy Lee 195

    Mary Jane Stanchina 207

    Lowell Gerson 217

    Frederica Cohen 227

    Ardith Keck 235

KECK NARRATIVES

    Emergency Medical System Formation — 245

    Addressing HIV — 251

    Combining Health Departments — 259

    Public Health Training — 269

    Federally Qualified Health Center — 277

    Above and Beyond — 293

REFLECTIONS

    Gregory Ervin — 303

    "Walter Evans" — 313

    Sue Phillips — 319

COLLABORATION CHECKLIST — 325

IMPRESSIONS

    Ardith Keck — 329

    David Kettlewell — 333

IN CLOSING — 339

BIBLIOGRAPHY — 343

ON COLLABORATION

INTRODUCTION

It seems a simple enough concept—to work together, to collaborate.

Like so much in life, there is more to collaboration than one might think at first glance or think is possible prior to experiencing a first collaborative effort.

It's not so much that collaboration is complex, although it can be, but more that, those who have spent their professional lifetimes engaged in rewarding collaborative efforts suggest that doing it well requires a unique grouping of skills and attributes.

Further, they say that by understanding the collaborative process in some detail, collaboration can be made easier, and your first steps in this type of teamwork will be more enjoyable for you and bring better results. I suppose that serves everyone's interests.

Thus, this book.

What will you find in the pages you now hold in your hands? You'll find a treasure trove of wisdom on collaboration from 15 experts representing a number of fields, the majority of whom are in public health. Shared themes come to light, providing verification on some level that a given idea is perceived as critically important.

Because of their generosity and gift of their lives' wisdom on collaboration, you can benefit from their aggregate experience and see first-hand what has worked and what has not worked for them. Their knowledge may be a useful guide to you in your exploration of and involvement in collaborative efforts. To their great gift, I've added some of my own thoughts on the principal themes

It is my hope, whether you are a first time or very experienced collaborator, that learning from and applying some of the lessons in this book will help you find success. This book can make a meaningful contribution to your enjoyment and success in life, based on the terms on which you define enjoyment and success. Surely, applying the skills and attributes of a good collaborator can help one navigate many of the parameters that portend success in other aspects of happy and healthy living.

WHY COLLABORATE?

Dr. Yuval Harari, Harvard scholar and author of *"Sapiens: A Brief History of Mankind,"* has spent the greater part of his career developing and sharing this intriguing idea: when you collaborate with others of your species, you will be harnessing the most significant and powerful dynamic responsible for the success of homo-sapiens on this planet. Harari says that our ability to create a shared vision and to work together on that vision to fulfillment over time has brought mankind to where we are as a species today.[2]

This is truly a thought-provoking statement. If you think about it, I believe you'll agree with me that most of our significant accomplishments (and I'll let you define them as you see fit) involve people working together with others to reach common goals.

Certainly, collaboration today has become a necessity in the field of public health, and, I suspect, in many other fields as well. For several decades public health professionals have seen their agenda expand while resources have declined. Thirty or forty years ago, how many of us would have predicted that we would one day be held responsible for controlling an epidemic of opioid abuse, stopping gun violence, or dealing with the social determinants of health —adequate housing, education, sustainable income, safe neighborhoods, and opportunities to exercise— to mention just a few?

---

[2] Harari, Yuval Noah. *Sapiens: A Brief History of Humankind*. New York, NY: HarperCollins, 2015. 31.

At the same time, we are living in a world of declining resources. This was a theme shared by many of our contributors, and I would guess that most Americans feel the same about many areas of endeavor. Whether you think about your social club, local volunteer work, or your job in a non-public health area, you perceive that often there is simply less money available to accomplish goals than in years past. This inability for a single agency, institution, or other group to reach a desired outcome on its own creates a level of stress that can only be dealt with by working with others. No one we communicated with believes this trend of diminishing resources in the area of human services will change in the near future.

Since the recession began in 2008, public health budgets have been cut substantially, and over 50,000 public health jobs have been lost across the US. Collaboration is now an essential mechanism for getting things done when the means or funding and expertise required are beyond what you possess. The common phraseology for this idea is one you already know so well: "You can get more done together than alone." Our contributors are unanimous in their belief that collaboration is the single most effective strategy they know of to get more done with less. I would add that collaboration is the most effective way to bring together the wide range of talent and physical resources required to solve many of today's problems and make services more accessible and effective. A real bonus is that collaboration often does not require new organizations, new employees, or buildings. Instead, a bit of repurposing allows existing organizational structures to accomplish meaningful goals.

We all have our own experiences and skill sets, but groups of people who have dedicated themselves to working together in a collaborative sense have more than multiple skill sets and experiences. They also have the ability to share best practices, to teach each other, and to draw on a wider range of knowledge than otherwise would be available to them. In other words, they become a true learning community, supporting each other in a manner that enhances their ability to think through problems, find solutions, and act together.

The contributors to this book and I have lived this truth, but we also must admit that working with others is not always easy, <u>for we must learn to see another's views and perspectives as equally valid to our own</u>.

It's worth taking a moment to reread the underlined portion —a couple of times!

A personal anecdote: My father was a physician, and as I sat next to him in the car and at patients' bedsides, he said, "Now Bill, remember that in any group of four people, there will be three you like pretty well, but maybe one you won't. Remember that your views are simply that—just your perspectives— and they only reflect your limited experiences. Life is bigger than what we see. Try to understand the other person—their needs, hopes and desires—and learn to focus on the good. And while you're at it, be kind about it, son. If you want to work at something, get outside of yourself and see the good in others."

Getting along well with others is central to success with collaborations. You may not like all those involved, and they may not all like you, but cultivating their trust and respect while providing the same for them is a necessity for success. You'll find the cultivation of effective interpersonal skills to be a prominent theme in the experiences described later.

There are many pragmatic arguments for pursuing collaborations, but personally, I like this reason best: it just plain feels good. Intuitively, I think we all feel that somehow, working with others is natural and good. It certainly makes us feel good to believe we can do so.

As I fathom my life to date, I would say that what I have done with others has brought the most joy to me, and perhaps many others would express similar sentiments. From my days as a child, to my time in school, to the Peace Corps, to a life in public health, now on a world stage in Cuba with their "rapprochement" with America, I feel best about what was done together in collaboration with others.

Thus, it may be said that collaboration somehow touches a *root* of humanity, something central to our being.

In this book, we'll walk you through success in collaboration in a step-by-step, organized way, although you know already that life itself is not quite so linear, as the stories from our contributors will reveal.

Ardith and I offer you our best wishes for all you do with collaboration and hope that this book will assist you personally and touch your life positively.

A QUICK DEFINITION OF COLLABORATION

There are many definitions of collaboration. The one I like best comes from the Wilder Research Center:

> Collaboration is a mutually beneficial and well-defined relationship entered into by two or more organizations to achieve common goals.
>
> The relationship includes a commitment to mutual relationships and goals; a jointly developed structure and shared responsibility; mutual authority and accountability for success; and sharing of resources and rewards.[3]

---

[3] Mattessich, Paul W., Marta Murray-Close, and Barbara R. Monsey. *Collaboration: What Makes it Work (2nd edition)*. St. Paul, Minnesota: Fieldstone Alliance, 2001. 4.

I would add to the second sentence that collaborators should also share the risks of their collaboration as much as possible. This all boils down to creating a more effective way to get your work done.

ARE YOU READY TO WORK COLLABORATIVELY?

Approaching the "how to's" of collaboration may seem a bit daunting, especially for someone new to the process. I don't think I can stress too much how important it is to carefully assess your own willingness and capacity to either lead or participate in a collaborative effort. Are you prepared to invest the time and effort that will surely be required? Are your interpersonal skills adequate for the task? Do you have the trust and respect of your potential collaborators? Can you see beyond yourself? Can you be flexible and adapt to new realities as the collaboration evolves? Do you have the patience to work with a diverse group of people? Do you have the support of your superiors? Do you have a good understanding of the community in which you are working? Do you think you might need some guidance? Do you have one or more trusted confidants you can solicit for help and opinions?

Time and Effort

When you read our contributors' stories, I think you'll be impressed by how much emphasis is placed on the need to spend the time required to work with others. The old adage, "If you want to go fast you should go alone, but if you want to go far you should go with others," is at the core of collaborative work.

Time is a precious resource, and collaborating successfully requires that you are willing to spend considerable amounts of it meeting with others to assess their interest in joining you, planning your work, and then carrying it out. A collaborative network may well require going "Above and Beyond," as we describe on page 293.

Interpersonal Skills: Building Relationships with Others

Put simply, people like to work with people they like, trust, and respect, and that means building and maintaining personal relationships.

Our contributors describe a variety of ways to do this, including talking on the phone, meeting for coffee or lunch, or engaging in some other social activity that allows you to spend time together and build a personal relationship. This simple idea often gets lost in the pressure of daily work and life activities.

Valuing others and getting to know others by investing your time in them does more than help you get results; it affects how collaborative efforts *feel* to you. That is also an important consideration. We all know people who have the reputation of not caring what others think or how they make others feel. That type of personality is not likely to foster good collaborations.

So try to manage things in a way that allows you to enjoy spending time with others. Our contributors say it makes everything more fun and gets better results too.

Trust and Respect

"Liking" your collaborative partners and being liked by them in turn is important, but probably not as important as having mutual trust and respect. Of course, academic credentials that you bring to the table create a first impression, but it is what you have accomplished, how you've accomplished it, and how you've treated people along the way that really impacts what others think of you. We've all known folks who seem to be very impressed by their own credentials and who believe they know best for everyone else. We don't really want to spend much time around them!

What are some of the characteristics that engender trust and respect beyond academic credentials? This is likely intuitive to most of us, but here are some abilities that our contributors and I can suggest to you:

- Displaying a positive track record
- Working diligently
- Proving consistency with words and actions
- Communicating openly and completely
- Listening carefully
- Showing understanding and empathy
- Sharing both credit and risks willingly
- Advocating inclusiveness
- Demonstrating humility
- Displaying patience and holding back anger
- Mediating skillfully

No doubt, you could easily add items to this list that resonate with you. Perhaps a single word to use in summary is *professionalism*. Wouldn't we all like to be considered the consummate professional?

Humility—Seeing Beyond Yourself

To put this another way, ask yourself if you can see beyond your selfishness. The greater part of a human being's life is determining in great detail what we believe in, what we think, and what we choose to do. It's part of the process of defining who we are throughout our entire lives. But in a collaboration, you are far more likely to succeed by mastering the art of learning what others think and feel.

The actual technique is fairly easy. It requires that you act with humility by avoiding strong expressions of your own position while asking yourself, "How do others feel and think, and why?"

An effective approach would be to:

- Ask their opinion
- Ask why they feel that way
- Ask relevant questions
- Take time to think things through—perhaps a day or more
- Consider the pros and cons of their views as you see them
- Consider how your views differ from theirs
- Come back together and talk about your thoughts on their views and ask for their response

The very fact that you give such careful consideration to their views will mean others will know that you are listening carefully and taking their thoughts seriously. The more time you spend considering other people's views, the better things will go for you in a collaboration.

Flexibility

You might also ask yourself how flexible you can be. As our contributors make clear, collaborations often operate in an extremely fluid environment. The more complex the issue and the more partners collaborating, the more likely there will be unanticipated twists and turns.

Responding well to those twists and turns can make or break your collaborative effort. Partners may come or go, funding sources may appear or disappear, collaborative partners may have a change of heart, and other external circumstances may occur that either help the collaboration succeed or interfere with its progress.

When these kinds of things occur, and they usually do, it's helpful to remind yourself of the purpose of the collaboration and avoid tying yourself to a specific pathway to success. Talk with your partners and explore the options available to respond to whatever the issue is. Others may be able to suggest alternative pathways that can increase the likelihood of success if you are willing to consider them

Patience

If you are a public health worker, it is likely you understand the meaning of patience. It often appears that little of substance happens quickly in public health unless it is something bad, such as a disaster or a disease outbreak. Other than responding to emergency situations or following the daily routines of clinics and inspections, we tend to be engaged in activities that are long range and time consuming. We don't improve a community's health status in a day, nor do collaborative activities tend to move quickly!

Collaborations tend to involve people who are diverse in profession, personality, and professional relationships. It takes *time* for people to consider ideas in sufficient detail to consider changing their opinion—days, weeks, and sometimes months. It takes *time* for people to learn to work together in a group, particularly if they are new to the process. It takes *time* for organizations to shift directions—sometimes years. And it takes *time* for us to change our thinking and develop new behaviors.

Exhibiting patience while interacting with others and while working to reach goals that may be complex is an attribute that brings significant dividends to collaborative efforts. "Keeping one's cool" is another prerequisite for success. It buys time to discuss and resolve points of difference. It helps to establish a group culture focused on respectful exchange of ideas and a resolve to find ways to make things work rather than to fail.

Support of Your Superiors

Working on a collaboration means your job description may change and/or the goals you are expected to reach in your position may be revised, so it makes good sense to be absolutely sure that your board or chief executive and management team are strongly supportive of the collaborative effort.

Present the pros and cons of the collaborative effort as best you can to those you report to and work closely with. Explain what factors make the collaborative effort likely to succeed and some of the problems you may face that could jeopardize the effort's success.

This last point is so important because a good rule to follow is: no surprises.

No one expects a guarantee of success, and certainly you're in no position to promise it, but you should accurately depict the situation as you see it.

Ongoing, direct communication with those you report to and work with is also essential. After all, the situation on the ground may evolve rapidly for better or worse. Everyone likes to deliver good news. If the news is good, you should deliver it, but it is just as important to deliver bad news to avoid surprises and to gain whatever guidance your superiors may have.

If you don't have the kind of relationship I've described here with those you report to, you may become leery of collaborative arrangements where you might not be able to control events as they change.

Knowledge of Your Community—Systems Thinking

One of the most important elements of building collaborative networks is having intimate knowledge of the various agencies and systems in your community that are relevant to the problem you are addressing, and being able to use that knowledge to gain understanding of how the community works and of the existing patterns of communication and services. This ability is called "systems thinking" and is defined by Peter Senge as follows:

Systems thinking is a discipline for seeing wholes. It is a framework for seeing interrelationships rather than things, for seeing patterns of change rather than static "snapshots"…[it is] a sensibility for the subtle interconnectedness that gives living systems their unique character.[4]

The central idea is to shift one's thinking from a reaction to the present to imagining and creating a desired future.

Are you a systems thinker? If you're not sure and want to understand this concept better, you should take a look at Peter Senge's book referenced in the footnote below.

Mentoring

Are you contemplating your first effort at collaboration? Are you part of a collaboration that is struggling—or even failing? Are you a bit intimidated by the responsibilities involved in leading a collaborative effort? Are you wondering if you have the skills and attributes to lead a collaboration?

The ability to participate in and/or lead a collaboration is like any other skillset; it improves with practice. If your experience is limited, it makes sense for you to seek and enjoy the benefits of receiving mentoring from others who are both experienced and successful.

Good mentors tend to be giving people. Approach them, explain your goals and needs, and ask for their assistance.

A good mentor can help you avoid common pitfalls and provide insights you would likely not have thought of on your own. They will challenge your assumptions, congratulate you, be a sympathetic ear, and most of the time, be a friend.

---

[4] Senge P.M., *The Fifth Discipline: The Art and Practice of the Learning Organization.* New York, NY: Currency, Doubleday, 1990. 68-69.

To select a mentor, find someone with direct experience in collaboration, typically older but not always so, whom you respect. Just ask them if they'd be willing to mentor you. You'll be surprised that most of the time they will agree to help.

Trusted Confidants

We always hope when we engage in collaborations that everyone involved will be respectful of each other, participate fully, share the vision for which the collaboration was formed, and agree with the direction the majority feel is appropriate. Unfortunately, I must tell you that in my experience, smooth sailing is less common than the opposite, especially if the collaboration is complex.

So many things can complicate the process. Some members of the group will be less likeable than others. Some may have a negative history with each other and come to the table nursing grudges. Some may not be convinced they should be part of the collaborative and find it difficult to participate wholly. Opinions about the best way to proceed may be quite different from each other and tightly held by their proponents. Unanticipated threats from the outside may threaten the purpose or activities of the consortium. And on, and on, and on.

These kinds of issues are quite common, and the consequences of making the wrong decision can threaten the integrity of the group and the process. If the group has evolved into a real learning community, many of these kinds of problems can be dealt with by discussing them thoroughly and developing consensus on the best approach, reminding each other that it is their thoughts that are in conflict, not themselves. Occasionally, however, the problems are more difficult to deal with, and possible resolutions can be fraught with the risk of unintended consequences.

A tool that has been extremely helpful to me in these kinds of situations is to discuss the problem "off line." I developed a small circle of trusted confidants whom I trusted never to speak of the issues with anyone else. Usually they were not members of the collaborative partnership, although on some occasions they could have been. Part of the bargain I struck with these folks was that I was seeking their advice in order to be sure I was seeing as many sides of the issue as possible and contemplating as many paths ahead as I could, but they should not hold me to agree with them and to follow their advice in part or in whole. They needed to be secure enough in their own egos to understand that as either the leader or just a participating member, I was responsible for trying to help the group decision-making process and only I could decide the best way for me to proceed.

After all, I was the one with the most complete picture of the situation, and I knew the most about the personal characteristics of the participants. If I chose not to follow their advice, it would not prejudice the relationship we had.

That process worked very well for me over the span of my career. This type of dialogue allowed me to become an observer of my own thinking. It allowed me to escape the emotion of the moment and spend time thinking the issue through while gathering valuable advice from people who were encouraged to speak truth to power with no ill consequences for them. My wife was always a member of this group, and my deputies and administrative assistants at both the health department and college of medicine were all occasional members, depending on the issue.

BUILDING A COLLABORATION

After assessing your readiness to participate in a collaboration and taking whatever steps you decide are relevant to improve your capacity, it is time to take the paths required to actually put the coalition together. In this section you'll find a description of the issues our contributors and I believe are the most important in that process.

Clear Understanding of What You Want to Accomplish—A Shared Vision

One of your first considerations when entering the world of collaboration—working together to reach a common goal—is what kind of goal is worthy?

You'll find that there are shared characteristics among the kinds of goals that are an excellent fit for collaboration. They tend to be those which are large in scope, involve expertise which you do not possess, have a long timeline, require financial and other resources beyond your means, or which, by their nature, require a larger sphere of contacts.

It is also our experience that the larger the social mission—the more others are served— the more likely your goal is a good fit for collaboration.

If the issue you are facing lends itself to a goal that is a good fit for collaboration, ask yourself, "Is this goal something that other people will see as critical to accomplish? Is it something they will believe in fervently and persevere with over time to see accomplished?"

Then ask others. Gather opinions from representatives of all stakeholder groups, and perhaps even from people not immediately involved who may, nonetheless, have important opinions to share. Do they feel it's a worthy goal? Are they interested? What do they think?

When you ask the question, listen closely to the answers. Ponder them carefully and avoid the tendency to dismiss opinions that don't match yours. Become skilled at considering other's opinions, both positive and negative, and not jumping to quick conclusions. Care in this area is one of the keys to success in collaboration and will also pay you dividends in your personal life.

Take some time to craft your vision of the intent of the collaboration. Put it on paper and practice sharing the ideas with others. Do not take communication for granted. Often, people do not really grasp what we are saying in the context in which we share it, so take your time and develop a clear presentation of the intent of the collaboration. Each time that you verbalize the goal(s) of the collaboration, your own understanding of the concepts will evolve and become richer, and the likelihood that others will share your vision increases.

Note that this ability for others to see your vision as valid and to act on that vision in concert is no small thing. Collaborations succeed and fail based on how clearly the vision is expressed and how widely it is shared by the participants.

Of course, you may realize that after carefully considering the intent of a potential collaborative effort and receiving feedback from others, you may come to the conclusion that it would not be wise or productive to move ahead. Don't be afraid to say *no*, to make the decision that a collaborative effort is not worth the time or effort required. Discernment and choice play the larger part of shaping our lives.

Be Clear About What You Bring to the Table

Public health is often resource poor, but your partners need to understand that you are reaching out to them for more than just access to their funding or authority. Public health agencies and professionals have a lot to offer to community partnerships, not the least of which is the moral authority that emanates from the only agencies (health departments) statutorily responsible for community health. You may very well bring the broadest vision of what is possible and be neutral ground where other competing agencies, such as hospital systems, can come together to reach mutually desirable goals.

Health departments have access to population data not easily accessible to others and often have the talent and expertise required to apply that information epidemiologically to best describe the nature of a problem and assess efforts to remedy it. Despite public health's relative poverty, you may also have access to facilities (meeting rooms, computer software, clinic spaces), funding (local, state, and federal grants), and talent (epidemiology, emergency planning, health education, environmental health) not present elsewhere. You also can bring a promise of so-called sweat equity to the group. Hopefully your partners will recognize from your history that you will work hard to make any endeavor you join to be successful so their investment in you and your project will likely be worthwhile.

The same applies to those readers who work in disciplines other than public health. Be clear about what you bring to the table so others will understand you will contribute what you have to create the compendium of resources the collaborative project requires to move ahead.

Keep Your Promises

A parallel point here is that when offers and promises are made to a partnership, it is critical that you deliver on them. This is a test of competence. Your long-term credibility as a partner depends not just on your ability to listen and talk but also on your ability to back up your words in ways that demonstrate your value.

Choosing Collaborative Partners

You'll want to give the same careful thought regarding who you bring into the collaboration effort as you did to what you want the collaboration to accomplish and whether it is worth doing. Or perhaps you will be looking at a collaborative effort already up and running which you've been asked to join. In either case, it is worth taking a careful look at actual or potential partners to assess their impact on the workings of the group.

There are two basic considerations here. First, which organizations or individuals must be included in the collaborative in order to have the highest likelihood of reaching the goals that have been set, and second, which individuals should represent the included organizations.

The "Power Pie"

Dr. Ricardo Martinez (see page 94) suggests that we look at the people and organizations we include in a collaborative effort as a "power pie," and he means pretty much exactly what the phrase conjures in our minds—a pie still in the pie pan which has been cut into slices.

So if you can keep this image in your mind, he explains that if you leave someone out of your collaborative effort who possesses a tremendous amount of influence (or power, as it were) that same individual will feel excluded, and in the time ahead will block the approval or implementation of your project if they can. I've seen what he described happen but had never really thought of the pie analogy.

It is respectful to include those people and groups who will be affected by what you do in your collaboration and in the actions and solutions you determine in aggregate to be appropriate. Leaving out an organization whose opinions should have been considered and respected is risky business indeed. It is very difficult, if not impossible, to get support for your actions from groups that are affected by your decisions but not included in their development.

Diversity

An element of that inclusiveness is paying attention to diversity when putting a collaboration together. We have the tendency when choosing people to work with to choose people who are like us—people with the same values, the same color, the same socio-economic status, and the same education. Perhaps they even live near us. We're often most comfortable with homogeneity.

The most effective teams, however, bring together people with very different views and skillsets representing the broad range of stakeholders for a project. Diversity goes far beyond race, which is its common interpretation. It might mean that you include representatives of the clients you are serving with your collaboration. For example, if you are working on a collaboration which addresses the health needs of a section of your community, include people who live in that community in your collaborative effort.

Collaborative Personalities

You'll want to choose, to the degree possible, individuals who are most likely to contribute positively to the work of the group rather than detract from it. If you've been asked to join an existing group, you'll need to review and assess the members while making a decision about joining.

The contributors to this book offered varying views on this question. Some said it was important that you enjoy and get along with fellow collaborators and discussed the benefits of social time together to build the relationship. Others said it was only necessary that you respect and trust your fellow collaborators. From my experience, both are valid perspectives.

First, I look for people who have a strong attraction to the intent of the collaboration. I want someone who feels as intensely as I do, as the road is not always easy, and the road is often long. This is critical. One has to stick with the collaboration long enough to see results, and I have found the ability to do this is directly related to their personal sense of or passion about the mission.

I have found that you do not have to have experience in collaborative efforts to be a successful collaboration partner. Motivation and interest with a willingness to learn and participate can trump experience. Experience helps, as in all things in life, but I wouldn't reject a potential collaborative partner due to lack of that person's track record in collaborative efforts.

Like most people, of course, I have a keen sense of enjoying the company of other people, and I can't help but look at things from that perspective as well. Some of our contributors hinted that people break into two principal groups: those who get along with others well and those who don't, inferring that one would be wise to work with those that do.

My father's advice comes to the fore again: I look for the good in others. There's a certain amount of acceptance of human foibles in all of this, and this acceptance is powerful. You may have to put a lot of yourself aside to accept things you may not be wild about in others in order to keep a collaboration functioning.

Not everyone who starts working in a collaboration remains until the goal is met, but I accept that as part of the process. People's lives change, and what may have been a good fit for them at the onset can change over time. And sometimes, people leave their places of employment for one reason or another.

Integral to this discussion is the truth that one cannot always pick who they will be collaborating with. Sometimes the collaborating partners come together in ways where you cannot choose or "vet" them but must work with them. In those cases it is up to you to do what you must to make the relationships work.

That said, I cannot remember a single instance in my years of collaboration where I was unable to participate in a collaborative effort due to personality issues alone.

Benjamin Franklin said, "Keep both eyes open before marriage, and one eye shut after."[5] Perhaps that statement has some applicability here. After all, the ability to accept other's foibles may help us to accept our own.

I always try to remember that my principal task is to make sure others respect, trust, and like me. A large part of that is being open to accepting them for who they are while I work to earn their respect and trust. That is just a nice way of saying, "Be the kind of person others want to work with, and perhaps you won't need to focus so much on whether they are a good choice."

MANAGING A COLLABORATION

Once you've assessed your own readiness to participate in or lead a collaboration and the collaborating entities have agreed on a shared vision for the work of the group, then the real work begins. In this section we'll describe the elements our contributors suggest are integral to managing the work of a collaboration.

Define Each Member's Role

As with any activity involving groups of individuals, things will go more smoothly if there are shared expectations for how your collaborative partners will work together over time.

Early decisions will include expected logistical considerations, such as who will lead the effort, how often you will meet, and what method will be used to keep each member aware of progress.

---

5 Franklin, Benjamin. *Poor Richard's Almanack*. New York, NY: Peter Pauper Press, 1981. 50.

Effective communication is absolutely key to success of a collaboration.

Think carefully and together about each of these issues. What is really best for your team? What is realistic given your schedules?

Decide who will keep minutes and prepare and distribute progress reports. Think ahead regarding what steps will be taken if a member does not participate.

Fortunately, most collaborations involve people with considerable managerial experience and good intentions, so these decisions are usually fairly straightforward.

Set Performance Benchmarks

As with any activity which takes place over large expanses of time, collaborative partners need to have a sense that meaningful progress is being made. The most effective way to do this is to set benchmarks early on, define what progress is expected by what date, and report it to all collaborative partners in a timely manner. These actions create real incentives to keep the effort on track.

Keep the Needs of The Group in Mind

A well-functioning collaborative becomes a "Learning Community;" that is, the group meets regularly, shares expertise, exhibits mutual trust and respect, and works collaboratively to reach a common goal. The individuals involved focus on the needs and progress of the group and work together to achieve its goals in an atmosphere of perceived fairness to all.

This is remarkably different from working alone. The mission of the group comes first, sometimes requiring that individual issues be subsumed for the good of the whole.

Let Your Ideas Go

One example of keeping the needs of the group in mind is to "let go" of ownership of your ideas that are embraced by the group. Allow others to take on your ideas as their own; let them speak of them as their own; and yes, perhaps permit them even to take credit.

This is difficult. After all, it was your idea! By the very nature of how we humans think, letting go of ownership of ideas makes sense. When we first hear an idea, we tend to discount it. Then in time, we see the validity, and then it is not uncommon for people to conclude it was their own idea in the first place.

People have the most buy-in and commitment to ideas which are their own. Actually, their taking credit for creating the idea serves your purposes if your goal is to serve. And of course ideas evolve over time, and others do contribute greatly to the development of the concept.

I've found it doesn't really matter whose idea it is—or was. Most important is that if it makes sense, it becomes operative for the group. "My," "me," "mine" can evolve into "we," "us," "ours." The less your work in collaborations is linked to ego, the better things will go for you and the group.

When Being Right Can Be Wrong

When working in a collaboration, you may find yourself in the middle of a situation where you know you are correct on a given question, but your view is not the predominant one. Having the strength of character to allow water to run its own course is necessary at times, especially on minor points.

Being right in your own mind has its place (of course you are passionate about your views), but recognize that others are also passionate about their views. The fact is things will not always go the way you want. Don't be afraid to compromise and proceed differently toward the same goal.

Simply put, by letting go of your need to be right or to have it your way, the flow of the group will be served. A good reference point is to ask, "What is good for the group?" and "Can I accept the ideas of others fully—and even support them—when they are not my ideas?" If the others' ideas are likely to move the work ahead, then insisting on your approach will be counterproductive.

Sharing Risks and Rewards

While it is true that in any group activity some participants will do "more" and some will do "less," it's important that all members of your collaboration feel they have been recognized and honored to some extent as you travel the road to success.

This is not so easy to accomplish, because often people will communicate something like, "You have really done something wonderful here," to one or two individuals as a personal compliment. In truth, the entire collaborative accomplished the goals, so be sure you say so.

The same goes for sharing the risks involved in a collaborative. Things may not always go well, and sometimes they might go quite badly. In those situations, if the collaborative is to survive, the risks and, if need be, the blame must also be shared. In my experience, if the risks and rewards are not shared, it is likely that one or more partners will leave the collaborative.

As in all human activity, it is easy to hurt another's feelings, resulting in people feeling left out or abandoned. The bad taste left in people's mouths may poison not only the current partnership but also the potential for future joint endeavors.

This seems to fit into the theme, "*less* of ourselves, *more* of others in thought and action."

Bringing on New Members

It may seem a bit overzealous to define what you will do when collaborative members depart and new ones come aboard, but it's all part of thinking ahead. Collaborative partners may come and go for truly valid reasons. Some may change jobs, and others may retire.

When they go, you'll likely bring in new collaborative partners, and they will need help to understand the vision for the collaboration and all the responsibilities that members carry. Make it easy to share it all. You might even consider the use of videos posted in a secure area on YouTube to share the vision of the collaboration with new members. However you manage it, give new members the help they'll need to grasp the big picture and learn the culture of the group.

Leaving a Collaboration

In our society, the very idea of quitting seems inappropriate, but our contributors indicated several instances when it is likely the right move. Of course, the most positive reason to leave a collaboration is that the goal has been met in full and a collaborative effort is no longer required. On that same positive track, your job may change, and your organization may need to select another person to replace you.

Or the reason may be more problematic. You may conclude that overall, the pattern of actions of the collaboration does not meet your personal ethical standards or those of your organization, for example. I empathize with those who face this quandary, because leaving a collaboration under those circumstances is not likely to bring you much of a feeling of having made a positive difference and may make future collaborative efforts more difficult.

Some of our contributors said they would leave a collaboration if they felt no progress was being made towards reaching goals and continued participation seemed valueless.

I do feel it's appropriate at the time you join a collaboration to give some thought to what circumstances might cause you to leave. Every castle needs a back door.

OTHER LESSONS LEARNED

Engage Others in the Vision from Top to Bottom in Your Organization

As we've noted previously, it is wise to keep your superior(s) informed, but it is just as important to keep the members of your own organization informed about the intent and general progress of the collaborative initiative. It is likely that the outcome of a collaboration will impact them to some degree. They may wonder if their jobs will change or even if they will have a job if the collaboration succeeds. Let people know what you're doing and why. They don't necessarily need to be actively engaged as a collaborator, but the work they do "back home" in their own silos should not only be valued but is also essential to the work of a collaboration. Be sure you help them understand the role they play in your partnership's activities and success.

Remember, you may need the support in both word and deed of your organization's staff to carry out the work of a new reality when the collaborative achieves its ends. We've included interviews with my former deputy director, Gregory Ervin (see page 303), and my former administrative assistant, Sue Phillips (see page 319) to show the benefits of involving key organization staff members in supporting collaboration efforts. It is clear to me that my successes would have been far fewer without their understanding and active participation in many of my collaborative ventures.

There are many ways to go about this, such as organizational newsletters, staff meetings, and email notes from the boss. What worked best for me was to utilize monthly staff meetings that almost every employee attended to explain what issues were impacting the agency, including any ongoing collaborative efforts. I liked this venue best because it allowed anyone in the audience, from top-level administrators to the janitors, to ask questions and make comments. I was able to squelch incorrect rumors and alleviate a great deal of anxiety in a number of cases this way. It gave people confidence that I would always be accessible and straightforward with them.

Identify "Champions"

Businesses, governmental organizations, social service agencies, educational institutions, and hospitals all operate under their own sets of policies and procedures. When these entities are part of a collaborative effort, it can be extremely helpful to have someone inside the organization who feels positively about both the work of the group and the role played by their organization to function as a champion for the collaboration's shared vision.

Ideally, this person(s) should be both a high-ranking decision maker in their own organization and a member of the collaborative group. An intimate knowledge of the inner workings, priorities, and personnel of an organization, coupled with the ability to direct some of the organization's activities, allows a collaborative champion to facilitate and support the organization's participation in and contribution to the collaboration. A champion can help by keeping their leadership informed and supportive, anticipating and mitigating potential problems with the work of the collaborative in their own organization, and securing resources from their organization to support the work of the group.

While it is certainly helpful to have an organization's leaders active in a collaborative effort, that is not always possible. Effective champions may also be found at other organizational levels. The "Walter Evans" (not his real name) narrative found on page 313 provides an example of how critical the work of a federal case officer was to gain the approval of his superiors for funding to support the development of a new federally qualified health center in Akron. The timely and artful use of persuasion resulted in a change of heart that allowed the project to proceed.

Identify a "Convener of Stature"

In their excellent book, *Finding Allies, Building Alliances: 8 Elements that Bring – and Keep – People Together,* authors Mike Leavitt and Rich McKeown lay out practical steps that leaders can take to form successful collaborations, even among competitors.[6] One of the important elements they discuss is what they call, "a convener of stature:" an individual, organization, or combination of the two with the stature to bring independent parties together to create something of value.

This was not an issue identified by our contributors, but I believe as you read their stories, you will note that they and/or their organizations clearly exhibit this trait. They exemplify the characteristics of effective conveners identified by Leavitt and McKeown, such as trustworthiness, a reputation for fairness, a broad sphere of influence, independence of thought and action, good diplomatic skills, skillful perception of motivators for participation, and some ability to create a sense of urgency to work together.

This may seem daunting to someone new to collaboration. Early in my own career I was able to use my title as director of health or chair of a medical school department to bring people to the table. To keep them there and maintain working relationships, I had to prove to them that I was dedicated to the task, could be trusted to listen to alternative views and be fair, and apply the resources at my disposal to support the effort.

---

6   Leavitt, Mike and Rich McKeown. *Finding Allies, Building Alliances: 8 Elements that Bring – and Keep – People Together.* San Francisco, California: Jossey-Bass, 2013. PDF e-book.

If you desire to form a collaboration or have been tasked by others to do so, assess your own strength as a convener of stature. If you have doubts about your standing in that regard, you may want to identify a co-convener (a person or organization) with sufficient "clout" to support your efforts.

Identify the Collaboration's Leader

The convener of a collaboration may be recognized immediately as the appropriate leader for the group if the convener is an individual, but that may not be the case. The convener may have the characteristics required to get others to commit to working together but may not have the time or temperament to actually lead the group's proceedings. As Hicks and Larson put it, "Sustaining the energies of group members and keeping them focused on the goals represents the essence of leadership."[7]

Talented collaborative leaders will behave as they wish the other members to behave. They will create a communication climate that allows any member to discuss any issue that may adversely affect the group's work, and they will address any issues that are identified. The ability to render at least some degree of thoughtful control over an enterprise is a prerequisite for successful collaboration.

What Is Perceived As "A Loss" May in Fact be "A Win"

As we've noted several times, collaborations don't always work out at all or work out as initially intended. This can be very discouraging, particularly if you and others have put a great deal of time and energy into trying to move the project ahead. I've never had the feeling, however, that a project that ended up being considered a failure had no redeeming qualities whatsoever.

---

7 Hicks, Darrin K. and Carl E. Larsen. *"Collaborating with Others."* in *Mastering Public Health: Essential Skills for Effective Practice*. eds Barry S. Levy and Joyce R. Gaufin, New York, N.Y.: Oxford University Press, Inc., 2012. 340.

By definition, a collaborative effort that doesn't finish successfully is not an individual failure but a group failure. That is one of the "shared" risks of collaborative ventures.

The experience of working together may very well have had some positive benefits on its own. You may have learned a great deal about a particular subject and about the workings of collaborations. You very likely developed new professional or even personal relationships that will stand you in good stead for future collaborations. The sense of shared loss can create its own sense of bonding with others and could result in a new resolve to tackle other problems together. Life is a circle, after all. If, as a result of participating in a collaboration, you have new relationships in place that help you help others in the future, this is success. These are "small" wins but are significant nonetheless.

There may be some "big" wins, as well. There were times in my career when I'd spent years working with a group towards achieving a goal and then watched things "go south." It appeared our vision would never be realized. In some cases, however, we were able to repurpose the effort to achieve a worthwhile related goal or to set the stage for future successful ventures.

The message here is that it is often possible to turn a negative event into a positive outcome. What we perceive as a "loss" can, in fact, actually be a "win." It requires an ongoing optimistic approach to work and life with a continuing search for alternate possibilities.

Going "Above and Beyond" the Norm
Why It's So Critical to Success in Your Career

As you move on to read about the experiences of our contributors, I think you'll be impressed by their resolve to do what it takes to achieve their goals. This resolve is more than just a willingness to work hard. That is a key element, of course, but it also indicates a willingness to step outside of the usual workday and to accept responsibilities implicit in moving a project ahead, but are outside of the person's expected range of activities. Our contributors are also willing to accept risks of failure that might otherwise be avoided.

In short, it means giving more than is required, going "above and beyond," if you will. It has been the hallmark of high-performing people since time began. Striving to reach excellence, going beyond what is required, brings out the best in us. I think it makes us stronger and wiser.

It's an attribute that comes with its own set of risks, however. I suspect we've all experienced people who are so driven that their personal life suffers in turn. From what I know of our contributors, I believe they have managed to find the right balance between dedication to work and dedication to the personal needs of self and family. Please take this as a cautionary note to find balance in your own life. Take the time to enjoy the life you have outside of your work and cultivate interests in other areas—family, music, literature, art, travel, exercise, hobbies—whatever it is that gives you pleasure and allows you to become a well-rounded human being.

THE SCIENCE OF COLLABORATION

The stories told by our expert contributors are informative but admittedly anecdotal and might be described as the "art" of collaborative practice. You might be wondering if there is any science to back up or support what we've told you. Yes, there is.

In 2001 the Fieldstone Alliance published the 2nd edition of *Collaboration: What Makes it Work*, the Wilder Research Center's analysis of collaboration research. This thorough analysis of the collaboration research literature at the time identified 20 factors that much of the research suggested could apply to collaborative efforts. These factors are grouped into six categories and are reproduced for you below:

Factors Related to the Environment

- History of collaboration or cooperation in the community

    A history of collaboration or cooperation exists in the community and offers the potential collaborative partners an understanding of the roles and expectations required in collaboration and enables them to trust the process.

- Collaborative group seen as a legitimate leader in the community

    The collaborative group (and by implication, the agencies in the group) is perceived within the community as reliable and competent—at least related to the goals and activities it intends to accomplish.

- Favorable political and social environment

    Political leaders, opinion-makers, persons who control resources, and the general public support (or at least do not oppose) the mission of the collaborative group.

Factors Related to Membership Characteristics

- Mutual respect, understanding, and trust

    Members of the collaborative group share an understanding and respect for each other and their respective organizations: how they operate, their cultural norms and values, their limitations, and their expectations.

- Appropriate cross section of members

    To the extent they are needed, the collaborative group includes representatives from each segment of the community who will be affected by its activities.

- Members see collaboration as in their self-interest

    Collaborating partners believe that they will benefit from their involvement in the collaboration and that the advantages of membership will offset costs such as loss of autonomy and turf.

- Ability to compromise

    Collaborating partners are able to compromise, since many of the decisions within a collaborative effort cannot possibly fit the preferences of every member perfectly.

Factors Related to Process and Structure

- Members share a stake in both process and outcome

    Members of a collaborative group feel "ownership" of both the way the group works and the results or products of its work.

- Multiple layers of participation

    Every level (upper management, middle management, operations) within each partner organization has at least some representation and ongoing involvement in the collaborative initiative.

- Flexibility

    The collaborative group remains open to varied ways of organizing itself and accomplishing its work.

- Development of clear roles and policy guidelines

    The collaborating partners clearly understand their roles, rights, and responsibilities, and they understand how to carry out those responsibilities.

- Adaptability

    The collaborative group has the ability to sustain itself in the midst of major changes, even if it needs to change some major goals, members, etc., in order to deal with changing conditions.

- Appropriate pace of development

    The structure, resources, and activities of the collaborative group change over time to meet the needs of the group without overwhelming its capacity, at each point throughout the initiative.

Factors Related to Communication

- Open and frequent communication

    Collaborative group members interact often, update one another, discuss issues openly, and convey all necessary information to one another and to people outside the group.

- Established informal relationships and communication links

    In addition to formal channels of communication, members establish personal connections—producing a better, more informed, and cohesive group working on a common project.

Factors Related to Purpose

- Concrete, attainable goals and objectives

    Goals and objectives of the collaborative group are clear to all partners, and can realistically be attained.

- Shared vision

    Collaborating partners have the same vision, with clearly agreed-upon mission, objectives, and strategy. The shared vision may exist at the outset of collaboration, or the partners may develop a vision as they work together.

- Unique purpose

   The mission and goals, or approach, of the collaborative group differ, at least in part, from the mission and goals, or approach, of the member organizations.

Factors Related to Resources

- Sufficient funds, staff, materials, and time

   The collaborative group has an adequate, consistent financial base, along with the staff and materials needed to support its operations. It allows sufficient time to achieve its goals and includes time to nurture the collaboration.

- Skilled leadership

   The individual who provides leadership for the collaborative group has organizing and interpersonal skills, and carries out the role with fairness. Because of these characteristics (and others), the leader is granted respect or "legitimacy" by the collaborative partners.[8]

---

8 Mattessich, Paul W., Marta Murray-Close, and Barbara R. Monsey. *Collaboration: What Makes it Work (2nd edition)*. St. Paul, Minnesota: Fieldstone Alliance, 2001. 7-10.

INTERVIEWS

This section of the book contains interviews of 15 individuals who are seasoned collaborators. They vary in discipline, gender, ethnicity, and seniority but share in experience with collaborations. Our interviewees illuminate the several dimensions of collaboration and represent outstanding resources for your review. We are grateful that, when asked to participate, they agreed.

C. WILLIAM KECK, MD, MPH, FACPM

Dr. C. William Keck (Bill) is professor emeritus and former chair of the Department of Behavioral and Community Health Sciences at the Northeast Ohio Medical University and former director of health for the City of Akron. He holds an MD degree from Case Western Reserve University and an MPH degree from the Harvard School of Public Health. He is past-president of the American Public Health Association, the Council on Education for Public Health, the Ohio Public Health Association, the Association of Ohio Health Commissioners, and the Summit County Medical Society. Dr. Keck currently chairs the Council on Linkages Between Academia and Public Health Practice and their Academic Health Department Learning Community, is vice chair of the board of directors of Medical Education Cooperation with Cuba (MEDICC), and is editor-in-chief of *MEDICC Review*.

Interviewer: Let's say you're giving a class on collaboration to a general public audience, not public health people. How would you answer the question, "What is collaboration?"

Bill Keck: I would say, in general, it's a tool that is available to folks who want to accomplish something that they can't manage on their own and they would need some help with. So it's a way to think about who else might share your interest, who else might share your vision of a different ending than you currently anticipate, and how you make that work—how you pull it all together.

Interviewer: Is the only operative precursor when considering collaboration the idea that you couldn't do it without someone else's help?

Bill Keck: No, it's the first one: you have to decide it's a goal you want that can't be reached without engaging others. Once you've made that decision, then you really have to assess a whole variety of factors in order to determine whether or not you're in a position where you're likely to be able to move ahead in a positive way.

You have to figure out who else might be interested in what you want to accomplish, particularly if they would like to see it done but can't do it by themselves, either. So, in other words, come up with a shared vision. Then you'd have to decide whether they're serious about this—as in, is there a champion who would bend their culture to reach a shared goal?

And then you need to assess the larger environment—how it would all fit, what impact it would have on the others, what kinds of resources would be involved, how you proceed in a way that is win-win, how you share the risks and share the rewards.

You really have to subvert your own ego and focus on the issue at hand rather than focusing on getting credit for it yourself.

> **"You really have to subvert your own ego and focus on the issue at hand."**
> —Dr. Bill Keck

And then you have to figure out how you're going to manage this and communicate with all the partners—how you're going to evaluate what you're doing and what you think will be the end result, so you'll know when to declare victory, or at least when to know whether or not you've achieved what you're after. And then you may have to decide just how you will share publicizing the results.

Interviewer: *Can you give an instance where a collaboration was not successful and why?*

Bill Keck: I tried to bring three local Ohio public health departments—Akron, Barberton, and Summit County—together, twice, without success. I worked my way into this by trying to take advantage of opportunities when leaders of other health departments retired and left. I thought that might be a good time to suggest we could do a better job of working together if we really were one agency.

I was able to convince the employed leaders that this was an issue worth exploring the pros and con's of, and was able to get some work done by various law departments and staffs to try to figure out what the complicating factors would be and what it would take to make this come about. But in most instances, I was unable to convince enough members of the board of health of one of those agencies that it was worthwhile doing, so it never happened, despite my best efforts.

Interviewer: Can you describe a situation when collaboration did work—where you decided to move forward?

Bill Keck: Let's piggyback on the above story. When it was clear that I couldn't move consolidation at that point, I asked myself whether it might be possible to realize some of the gains I was hoping would come about with consolidation by working in a more collaborative mode. If I could find some ways to help these three health departments work together on a number of projects, then maybe over time, the stage would be better set for an eventual consolidation.

So I pursued that avenue at the same time I was working with the boards of health trying to get them to consider merging. I was able to bring the leadership of the three departments together to make a pitch that we could do a better job of caring for and improving public health in the county if we found a variety of ways to work together starting with two major tracks. One was to develop programming that erased the geographic boundaries between us; another was to combine resources to look for funding from others for collaborative programming involving all three health departments.

Pragmatically, that meant we got our medical staffs together and decided that instead of asking people precisely where they lived to determine whether or not they could attend our clinics, that all of our clinics would take anyone from the county, and we would unify our medical policies and procedures. Further, we would suggest to patients that they go to the clinic that was most convenient or comfortable for them.

That meant that all of us were taking care not only of the bulk of people from our own geographic area but also some from other geographic areas. And of course, this got our medical staffs working together to create a unified set of medical policies and procedures. We would have had to do this if we were going to consolidate health departments, so why not do it ahead of time and have that already done?

Another issue that fit this model was infectious disease reporting, which was difficult in our county. We had four hospital systems and hundreds of physicians required by state law to report certain diagnosed communicable diseases to the health department where the patient lived.

We knew our reporting rates were comparatively low. When we looked at it, we found it was extremely confusing to people who wanted to report because sometimes when we asked a patient where they lived, they'd give an Akron address, but it was technically in another community. Some addresses in the suburbs of Akron are listed as Akron addresses, but they are actually in Summit County, so it could be very confusing about which health department to call. Most physician practices, even some of the hospitals, just weren't going to take the time to figure it all out and make sure the report went to the correct health department.

So we decided we should create one reporting system and that we would combine our staffs. The Akron Health Department had a physician who was our disease control medical officer, and the Summit County Health Department had a better computer system. We organized things in such a way that we created one number to call to report communicable disease anywhere in the county. That number reached the physician in the Akron Health Department who decided what the appropriate response should be and which health department or departments would respond. All three departments were connected to the communicable disease tracking system on the county health department computer system. If we had an outbreak that involved more than one geographic unit, we would combine our resources to deal with that issue together.

Our reporting rates went up, and I think our effectiveness in communicable disease control went up as well because we simplified the reporting and had a coordinated response that had us acting as if we were one department rather than three.

Interviewer: *So if I understand the story correctly, consolidation of the three into one didn't occur formally, but you did have consolidation of effort in a way that you hoped would be a precursor to a true consolidation.*

Bill Keck: Yes. To finish the story, we also did this for funding. We approached sharing funding in several ways. The first was to look for ways to share external grants. Because Akron was the larger health department and had an inner city area that had more significant public health problems than most of the other communities in Summit County, the Akron Health Department became preeminent in getting federal and state grants.

The three health directors decided when federal block grants were developed that we would apply for them as a county. We actually worked together to develop single funding applications based on the needs of the county rather than the needs of the jurisdiction of each health department. That strengthened our application and simplified the application process. The Ohio Department of Health was responsible for distributing federal block grant funds and really liked that approach. They encouraged us to continue.

It meant that Akron ended up giving up some of the funds that it would normally have had to itself in order to share them more widely. The result was not only more efficient and effective public health services but also the reputation that we could be trusted as a collaboration partner to share resources.

It also allowed the three health directors to go as a group to the hospitals in the area to develop a second funding stream. We were able to convince the hospitals that they should share some resources with us to address issues that they also had concerns about, such as prenatal care and childhood immunizations. We sat down with them and had three health departments and four hospital systems all working together looking at these problems. We were able to jointly decide on the best approach to take with the result that the hospitals provided funding for programs that the health departments carried out.

These collaborative working relationships got the three health departments working together in a way that eventually made the consolidation easier when it did finally happen, about four or five years ago now.

Interviewer: *Would you say that early on, resistance to consolidation was based on the fact that if you have three organizations with three leaders, and you're going to have one organization with one leader, at least two leaders are let go?*

Bill Keck: They are either let go or given responsibility that isn't at the top. Yes, so you have to work that out. There's also a strong history of home rule in Ohio, and I think the boards just wondered what would happen to them and their involvement if this consolidation worked. You don't need three boards after consolidation, so the board would have to be reshuffled. Some of them would lose positions that I think were important to them, so all those human factors need to be addressed as you proceed.

And the administrative systems really are quite different. The difference between a city and a county in Ohio is significant in terms of elements like hiring practices, employment rules, promotion, and salaries. All of those complications act at counter purposes and tend to slow people down when they contemplate how much work it will take to really merge three departments into one entity.

(Note: The topic of health department merger is explored further in Narrative #3 starting on page 259.)

Interviewer: *Are there things happening in the United States or in the global community today that you think make the need for collaborative efforts more pressing?*

Bill Keck: Sure, lots of things. The world is much more complicated than it once was. The interactions among groups are enhanced, and resources for many areas are not keeping up with the demands. Certainly, the public health agenda keeps expanding, while the funding, at least over the last decade, has been gradually declining.

We also find that if we really want to deal with today's public health problems, we have to include sectors and issues that typically haven't been part of the public health or the medical world—like mental health, drug use, housing, education, violence, and all the other social determinants of health. To deal with them you really need a large consortium. You need people with the skills that relate to those areas, and you need to find ways to bring all these various financial and organizational silos closer together, aiming eventually—it would be nice—to have a global budget for public health instead of all these little silos with all the different organizations, all the different rules, and all the different sources of funding. It's very hard to bring that together—sometimes impossible.

Interviewer: *What are three things that need to happen for collaboration to work?*

Bill Keck: First is shared vision. You need others besides yourself to agree that a goal you have in mind is worthwhile.

Second, as I said earlier, you need champions in potential partner organizations who are willing to think differently, to do some systems thinking together, to come together as a learning community to look carefully at all these issues, and move their own organization within the consortium in a way that allows the collaboration to occur.

Third, you need to find ways to share the risks and rewards. You have to share the work, ensure it is as evenly distributed and as appropriately distributed as possible, and that people get credit for what they do. If you're the leader of the group, you probably take less credit and give credit to others. So you reward others for working together as much as you can.

> **"You have to share the work and ensure . . . that people get credit for what they do."**
> —Dr. Bill Keck

Interviewer: Suppose that a public health organization is independent and chooses to go into a collaborative effort with another entity, but the bonus structure for the leader of the public health organization—the continuance of their employment, retention of salary and bonus structure— is based on meeting an assigned set of goals which were defined by the board in the prior year. Does the fact that you are diluting your role in providing public service to two organizations make it more difficult for the leaders of the entities collaborating to justify their salaries to their own boards? It seems that accountability of leaders meeting goals set by the board might become more complex.

Bill Keck: It's not easy. Part of the answer to that is to bring your evaluators along with you. [They have full knowledge of actions taken and goals defined.] For leaders in public health departments, it's the board of health; in hospitals, it's their own boards or their own chief executive if you're dealing with someone at the departmental level. They need to be on board. They need to understand what it is you're trying to accomplish.

Yes, it is a little riskier because you don't have full control, and yes, it might fail—and you need permission to fail. You need to have a group following you who will hopefully know whether you tried your best and not punish you unduly if it fails. However, sometimes it fails because the leadership is poor, and that needs to be evaluated as well.

Interviewer: So the answer to the question is . . .

Bill Keck: It depends!

Interviewer: So you need to amend your employer's expectations, perhaps redefine your role, and have a variety of indices defined by which all agree that you will be judged. Is that how you address that?

Bill Keck: I think so, yes.

Interviewer: Can you identify any reasons why people have been dead-set against collaboration?

Bill Keck: Well, of course it depends upon the circumstances and the personalities involved. There are some folks who just aren't very good at working with others, aren't really happy to do it, and really want to work by themselves. It's very difficult to collaborate with someone who's not interested—probably impossible.

> **"It's very difficult to collaborate with someone who's not interested— probably impossible."**
> —Dr. Bill Keck

Interviewer: What can you tell me about the mindset of someone who's successful at collaboration?

Bill Keck: First, you need someone who really sees the big picture, and you need a systems thinker who's able to evaluate the issues being faced and the resources available in general to deal with them. That person also needs to parse out from that what they're in control of and what they're not in control of, and to have some early thoughts about what might be possible if others were able to work with them.

So you need that global view of what potential possibilities there are.

Then you need someone who's willing and able to convince others that what they have in mind makes sense. To do that you really need to look at the other organizations and the people involved and do a mental evaluation of where you think the best potential lies for partnership, in terms of available resources and people with personalities who might be willing to work with you.

Again, systems thinking is certainly one part, along with having that global view, being willing to share all of the responsibility and outcomes with others, a willingness to subvert their own ego to the good of the group, and perhaps even to push others in the group more forward than themselves in terms of recognition should there be some success in all of this. A little humility can be quite helpful.

And then you need someone who can communicate well, track progress, and solve people problems.

Interviewer: *What percentage of people that are in leadership positions really have the mindset of a collaborator? Is it 10%, 20%, 30%, 50%, 70%?*

Bill Keck: It's probably a bell-shaped curve in terms of peoples' ability to do this, to have the right mindset. There are some, at least in my experience, that get it right away and say, "Yes, we can do this together."

There are some who say, "I can't really do that."

I think the majority is somewhere in-between, where they can be brought along, to one degree or another, depending on what the potential gain is from the collaboration and how much they are willing to put into the effort. I can't quantify it further, though.

I've been fortunate in my own experience to be able to find people in most cases that wish to do this. I've been thwarted a few times, but most of the time I've been able to find people who are willing to give it a try.

Interviewer: *It seems that the center section of your bell curve is made up of those who are willing to give it a try. Does having a mentor who is a more experienced, older individual, or one who is gifted at collaboration at a younger age, make a difference on the ability to get that center section bell curve to a successful outcome?*

Bill Keck: I believe so. It's like any other skill or set of tools. The more experience you have with collaboration, the more you are aware of the advantages and disadvantages of it. It's more likely that you'll anticipate and deal with problems as the process moves along, and the more likely it is you'll be helpful and that the collaboration will be successful.

Sometimes you need to teach folks who are reserved about this but willing to try it. With the right kind of work ethic and the right kind of personality, you can have real success. So yes, I've seen some people that have worked with me and then gone out on their own to arrange their own successful collaborative efforts.

Interviewer: *What can you tell me about the human ego as it relates to collaboration?*

Bill Keck: Certainly, you need to be reasonably sure that you're capable of doing this work, so that's some ego I guess, having a personal sense the needed skills are there.

But then at the same time, you need to be able to subvert that ego to include others. If you have a true partnership, then things are shared, and the sharing means you're not always out front. So it means sharing the credit, and it means when there are problems, you work together to solve them. You become a learning community, if you will.

Interviewer: Doesn't that mean you need to find new ways to find satisfaction in interactions?

Bill Keck: Well, if not new ways, at least you need to learn to be satisfied—more satisfied in the long run than the short. It's not like medicine where if someone comes in with pneumonia and you give them a shot, they get better. That's immediate gratification.

In collaborative arrangements, the short-term gratifications tend to be process oriented. Yes, they are willing to work with me; yes, we have figured out how we are going to organize and govern this; yes, we know how we're going to communicate; yes, we've decided how we're going to evaluate, and so on. It might be years before you will actually be able to see the results of your work and a change—in public health status in my case, or a different product in any other sphere of collaboration.

I think it means understanding that you need to modify the self-gratification requirements, look at small accomplishments along the way first, and wait—be willing and able to wait for the final acclimation if you are successful.

> **"You need to modify the self-gratification requirements, look at small accomplishments along the way first and wait—be willing and able to wait—for the final acclimation if you are successful."**
> —Dr. Bill Keck

Interviewer: Is marriage collaboration?

Bill Keck: I sure think it is. It's certainly teamwork, but to some degree it's collaboration as well. Maybe it's more teamwork than collaboration. I'm not sure. Certainly, two people together should be able to accomplish more than one on his or her own.

If you're going to be working in a collaborative mode in other places, a spouse can be very helpful, particularly if they also are working in collaborations of their own in the same or different field. Almost always there are sets of problems that arise as collaboration efforts move on, and it's valuable to have someone that you can talk over these issues with privately, out of the public eye, where you can feel free to lay your soul bare about the problems you are facing and maybe get some help or, at the very least, support.

RON BIALEK, MPP

Ron Bialek has been serving as president and chief executive officer of the Public Health Foundation (PHF) since 1997. He has focused PHF's efforts on developing and implementing innovative strategies for improving performance of public health agencies and systems. Initiatives include developing the consensus set of Core Competencies for Public Health Professionals through the Council on Linkages Between Academia and Public Health Practice and creating the most comprehensive public health learning management network in the United States—TRAIN. He is an editor of *Public Health Improvement Handbook* and *Solving Population Health Problems through Collaboration*.

Interviewer: *If you were explaining the topic of collaboration to someone unfamiliar with the topic, what would you say?*

Ron Bialek: To me, collaboration is the art of bringing together people with different views and different perspectives, identifying common ground and common interests, and being able to advance what emerges as common needs.

Interviewer: Do you think collaboration is a talent, or is it a skill you can acquire over time?

Ron Bialek: I think it's a skill you can acquire. Collaboration requires a lot of observation, a lot of listening, and a lot of humility.

Interviewer: Talk to me about humility.

Ron Bialek: If someone believes they have all the answers, they're far less interested in collaborating. Humility is portraying to others that you have much to learn. You are genuinely interested in hearing what others have to say and discovering what others do—even learning who they are as individuals. Sometimes you may even need to be a bit self-deprecating to open up doors and discussions. It's important to remember that as a collaborator, I'm simply a cog in a bigger wheel.

I have a role; you have a role, and humility is recognizing that there are lots of different roles and that none of us individually can really make the difference we might want to make.

> **"It's important to remember that as a collaborator, I'm simply a cog in a bigger wheel."**
> —Ron Bialek

Interviewer: Do you believe the sum of the whole is larger and greater than the individual parts?

Ron Bialek: Absolutely.

Interviewer: Why?

Ron Bialek: I look at a field like public health as if it were an organism. There are different parts of the organism that have to work together, and every part has a role. Collaboration is the same type of thing. You have to recognize that there are many parts that make up a whole—many pieces to every puzzle.

Interviewer: *What are the plusses of humility?*

Ron Bialek: Stephen Covey talks about making deposits into your "emotional bank account" by keeping promises and being honest, kind, loyal, and apologetic. I see some of the deposits as giving others emotional support, recognizing when you're wrong, and sucking it in even when you're right but the other person needs to be validated. You're making these deposits into this emotional bank account, and at some point you need the people you've made all the deposits with to let you withdraw some because *you* may need the extra support, and you may need their understanding. You may be encountering difficult times.

I think a lot about making those deposits—both professional and personal. I hope I'm a humble and honest individual; I think I am. If I'm not, it would be far more difficult to make deposits into that emotional bank account. If I'm regularly making deposits, when five years from now I need to get somebody to support a position I have, and I ask them for a favor, they may not question what's behind it or why I need it. They might just say, "Gee, I trust you, and you're asking for this, so I'm going to do it."

Interviewer: *Do you think that people sometimes have a tendency to say, "Okay, my personal life is my friends and family, but my business is a Ferrari, and it's got tractor treads on it, and I can grind up people on the way"? There almost seems to be a disconnect between the persona of the human being in a personal relationship and the persona of the human being in a business role.*

Ron Bialek: I find that people who are this way either don't enjoy what they're doing or get themselves into trouble, and I can describe my own personal experience with this. I've always been someone who puts all my cards on the table. I don't feel there's much benefit to holding them close to my chest. So here it is:

I move to DC, and now I'm running an organization, the Public Health Foundation. I put all my cards on the table when dealing with people, and some people who wanted to see my organization fail and ultimately fold wondered, "What am I holding back?" because here in DC people always hold something back. What am I holding back? Nothing.

I rather quickly—and ultimately wrongly—assessed that I better hold onto some of my cards, so that's precisely what I did. I spent maybe a month or so only showing some of them—and I went home every night feeling worse and worse.

Interviewer: And by "holding my cards," you mean you were not expressing what you felt?

Ron Bialek: It wasn't only that I wasn't telling them everything; I was just not exposing my organization or myself to vulnerabilities. If you lay everything out, you may be exposing yourself and making yourself vulnerable.

Interviewer: Would a vulnerable statement be something like, "Hey, this might not work!"—some kind factual statement that everybody knows but nobody wants to say. The emperor has no clothes, but you actually say that the emperor has no clothes.

Ron Bialek: Right, or "Gee, I'm not sure."

Interviewer: "I'm not sure." You're supposed to a leader; the world feels you're not supposed to be "not sure."

Ron Bialek: Exactly, so I was holding back, and I just started really hating my job and not really liking myself. And I finally decided I'm not that person. I can't be somebody completely different in my job.

Interviewer: Are you telling me that you have to be genuine to do collaboration?

Ron Bialek: [He laughs.] Yeah, I think you do.

Interviewer: It's not a stage show?

Ron Bialek: No, no. I actually tell this to my staff, and when I was at Hopkins teaching, I used to tell this to my students. You spend an entire career developing your credibility, and it takes a moment [snaps fingers] to destroy it. Is it worth it?

So be genuine; be honest; be upfront. It takes a long time to develop trust and credibility, but it's worth it in the long run.

> **"Be genuine; be honest; be upfront."**
> **—Ron Bialek**

Interviewer: So you're saying that people can sense or smell "genuine" and that you will get better results if you say what you believe in a respectful way.

Can you share some instance where you accomplished something through humility—something that reflects, "I think this is why it worked"?

Ron Bialek: Knowing precisely why something worked is always the tough part. One of my annual performance measures established by my board we call the Wayne Gretsky measure—skating to where the puck's going to be. My board asks me to describe how I anticipate what is going to be happening so we can position the organization in the field, effectively collaborate, and achieve mutual goals.

There are a couple of examples that come to mind. A number of years ago, as an activity of the Council on Linkages, we concluded as a group that in our field there's a lot of research that's not particularly relevant to what people are doing in practice. And we thought that there is a desire and a need for something we began calling public health systems research.

Funders and others really didn't know what we were talking about or weren't really supportive of this type of research. We acknowledged that we needed guidance from the field and said to potential funders that we'd like to give them a public forum to talk about their vision of how their organizations can help us in the field do what we need to do, and have the types of evidence to help do the right things.

For several years we invited some of these opinion leaders to national gatherings, such as the American Public Health Association annual meeting, gave them a public forum to talk about themselves, and to talk about what they were going to do.

Interviewer: *It was a talking collaboration.*

Ron Bialek: It was talk, and by asking them a few questions in advance, we wanted them to think about a perspective they had not thought about before because they would be talking about it publicly. And here's what happened over the course of about two or three years. The first year was, "Here's our thinking;" the second year was, "Here's what we're now thinking about doing;" and the third year was, "Here's the funding that we're putting out there for the community to do what we think is helpful in this new field of public health systems research."

So Bill Keck and I had this idea; we didn't know quite how to move the field forward, but we knew we needed to try. We knew, "We're not going to fund research like this, but how do we get those who are in those positions to fund it to believe it?"

So we helped the idea of public health systems research become their idea, and maybe that's really the key—not owning the idea.

> **"Maybe that's really the key—not owning the idea."**
>
> —Ron Bialek

I learned this actually in my public policy degree program: my job was to make my boss look good. If you really want to be successful and you want to get your ideas and perspectives advanced, if you can make them somebody else's idea—and a higher up's idea—it's going to move things forward more quickly than if you own the idea.

> **"If you really want to be successful and you want to get your ideas and perspectives advanced, if you can make them somebody else's idea—a higher-ups' idea—it's going to move things forward more quickly than if you own the idea."**
>
> **—Ron Bialek**

Interviewer: How do you go about making someone you're working for look good and have them view the ideas as their own?

Ron Bialek: It goes back to what you mentioned a while ago, which is listening. What are the needs, the ambitions, and the desires of the person who is the decision maker? What is it that that individual is looking to accomplish? What pressures does that individual have, and what pain does that individual feel?

When I used to work in state government, that's sort of how I approached my own boss—listening to what she was confronted with, and then if I had some ideas I was looking to advance, frame them in a way that she could see how it might help her and her cause. Then ultimately, a week or two later, she said, "Well Ron, why don't we do X?"

I'd say, "That's a good idea. I'd be happy to do X!"

Interviewer: It sounds like you're talking about realizing that the first time around the block, somebody might not recognize an idea too clearly, but after some time passes, all of a sudden their subconscious mind pushes a door open, and they can see it.

Ron Bialek: Yes. However, if it's not framed in a context of what the individual needs, their pressures, and their interests, I don't think they're ever going to see it. And that's where the listening really comes in. How can I advance something through someone else?

Interviewer: Have you ever been part of a collaboration that was an abysmal failure?

Ron Bialek: Yes. We were brought into and asked to participate in a collaboration to try to improve performance in the field of public health. It really turned out to be a single organization with its own particular agenda bringing together 10-15 other organizations all with their own agendas, and basically everybody came to the table with, "How can I advance what I want to do? How can I walk away with more money?"

The whole collaboration was really set up as a "You Win/I Lose."

Interviewer: So it was a grouping of personal agendas.

Ron Bialek: Absolutely.

Interviewer: And in that mix of personal agendas, there was no shared anything other than that table. They did sit at the same table. That had to be tough. Did you recognize that this was ploughing into the ground early on?

Ron Bialek: Unfortunately, yes. You might ask, "Why did you even show up?" I showed up to something like that because not showing up could result in more damage. So it was one of those situations where you show up just so you can be treading water and staying in place.

Interviewer: *Do you have other coaching for people on collaboration?*

Ron Bialek: Find a good mentor. There are others who are wonderful collaborators and wonderful sharers. And I've been fortunate to work with those individuals and to observe them—Bill Keck being one. I was also mentored by a gentleman who unfortunately passed away a few years ago, Moe Mullet. He was another truthful, trustworthy, and humble collaborator. It's amazing what you can learn from observing.

"Find a good mentor."
—Ron Bialek

Sometimes you can doubt the merits of collaboration. Sometimes you can become disillusioned, and it's very helpful to have mentors—people who you can look at, who you can observe, who you can call on and say, "Hey, I really could use your help," or sometimes it's even helpful just seeing that somebody who really stuck with it was able to make a difference.

I think mentorship is really key.

Interviewer: *Do you have a feel for the main reason why some collaborations fail?*

Ron Bialek: Lack of vision. There's immediate gain, and then there's long-term gain. If you're just looking at what's right in front of you, you may not need to collaborate today, or even at this moment, but in the long term, if you really want to advance a particular objective, and if you really have a vision for the future, collaboration is often key.

So if you don't have vision, you may not see the merits and rewards of collaboration.

Interviewer: Have you noticed what characteristics really good collaborators share? What can you tell me about the best of the best?

Ron Bialek: Sense of humor, a sense of fun in what it is they do, conveying a sense of "I want to help others," and honesty.

Interviewer: Do you think the need for collaboration today is greater than it was?

Ron Bialek: I don't know if it's greater than it was; I think it's something that doesn't exist nearly as much as it may have in the past. Today, there's much more "digging in;" there's much more "I have the answers;" there's much less honest discourse. Part of having or recognizing that you and I may have different opinions is accepting that your opinion is valid. Your opinion should be respected and discussed versus being dismissed. I think we're much more inclined to be dismissive today.

Interviewer: Why?

Ron Bialek: In part it may be the access to information—the information overload in some ways. You have so much information at your fingertips that people today can pretty much find someone or some group to validate their own opinions and thoughts and to reinforce whatever they are thinking as being right. And then if I'm sitting down with you in a community setting, I don't really need to listen to you because I already know what's right. Others have already validated it as I was searching online.

RICARDO MARTINEZ, MD, FACEP

Dr. Ricardo Martinez is the chief medical officer for Adeptus Health and is a nationally recognized, board-certified emergency physician. He has practiced emergency medicine clinically for more than 30 years and held senior roles in business, academia, and the federal government.

Interviewer: What are your general thoughts on collaboration? Why collaborate?

Ricardo Martinez: That's easy. The problem is too big, and the resources are too small. That's number one. If you look in terms of public health, we way underfund that in the United States. We basically have our healthcare focus on the demand side, not on decreasing demand.

Why collaborate?

"That's easy. The problem is too big, and the resources too small. We way underfund public health in the United States."

—Dr. Ricardo Martinez

So the real question is how to best enable a mission. Collaboration becomes key. As the saying goes, "If you want to go fast, go by yourself; if you want to go far, bring a team." It all starts with building that team.

For most of these problems, they're multidimensional, and there are a lot of stakeholders in place. The idea is to bring people around a shared vision, and by working with various people and their different capabilities, what you create is really a lot more effective approach to solving the complex issues in our society.

Interviewer: *As you look ahead to the next 20 years, do you see an increasing or decreasing need for collaboration?*

Ricardo Martinez: I think it's going to be increasing, and it's actually going to speed up dramatically. The growth of big data is doing that already because that tool is having us begin to view the world differently. We see connectivity that we didn't see before.

You can go back historically and see how better information changes how we think. I'm from Louisiana, and there were always the stories of hurricanes that arose with a darkening of the sky, increasing winds and sheets of rain, and then devastating the area and population. To observers, it was that "big storm came out of the East" sort of thing.

Then we invented and deployed the satellite and could see these hurricanes forming off the coast of Africa and coming across the ocean. We began to learn more and more about the time of year, how they were formed, and where they're coming from and be able to track them. It allowed us to see the connections between currents and weather and all these different things. No more surprises.

Increasingly, we're seeing different parts of society beginning to understand how they are connected to other parts. A good recent example is the greater focus on the linkage between transportation and health. In my government role, my focus was more on the safety side of transportation.

But now, we're also looking at things that affect health like sidewalks and bicycle lanes, how transportation affects readmissions for hospitals, and whether people can even access medical care. That's all happening because we're beginning to pull in data from isolated streams and get a greater insight into the big picture. The growth of big data is creating much greater awareness of the need to bring in all these various stakeholders around a central theme.

> **"The growth of big data is creating much greater awareness of the need to bring in all these various stakeholders around a central theme."**
> —Dr. Ricardo Martinez

Interviewer: *I see that you are the chief medical officer of North Highland Worldwide Consulting, which is a global consulting company.*

Ricardo Martinez: Yes. This role allows me to work with payers, health systems, clinicians, and national and international governments.

Interviewer: *What's the difference between the process of collaboration on a worldwide basis versus on a local basis?*

Ricardo Martinez: That's a good question. I can tell you that when I worked in my federal role, I routinely worked at both the national and local levels to introduce safety programs. Because I regulated the automotive manufacturers, which was going from a more national to global industry, I also had to deal with multiple countries. The difference really is just a matter of scale, to be quite honest with you, and in my view, it requires more complex politics.

But everything starts with a clear vision or a clear understanding of the problem.

People don't naturally do that. There are so many different issues that cross your threshold on a daily basis. Just read *The Wall Street Journal* or *The New York Times* front to back, and you'll probably get 70 different pressing issues out there.

So how do you get people to focus on a particular issue and have them think not only that it is important but that it's also something they can do something about and that they can make a difference?

And it's really those three things. First, it's got to be important. Second, it has to be something that they feel that they can do something about, because there are a lot of things that I read about that I can't do a whole lot about. Third, if I go and am successful in my efforts, can I make a difference? You have to feel that your actions will be meaningful.

And those three things draw people together around an issue.

> **"What will bring people together in a collaboration?**
>
> **1) It's got to be important.**
>
> **2) It has to be something they can feel they can do something about.**
>
> **3) If I go and am successful in my efforts, will it make a difference? You have to feel that your actions will be meaningful."**
>
> —Dr. Ricardo Martinez

With this in mind, start first with a clear understanding of the problem.

From the public health perspective, one of the things I truly believed was that every parent has the right to know what was killing the children in their community. And it was really interesting to realize how few people even knew. That was because the data was in silos: some of the data is here, some of the data is there, and some of the data is elsewhere.

It goes back to the idea of saying, "Wait a minute! Let's put all that data together and formulate the big picture." What that allows us to do is to understand and focus on what's killing our kids. Then it allows us to have a lot more stakeholders involved, because we now have a shared view and can talk about how we're going to address that.

On a global initiative, you have to find things that are crosscutting, whether it's the Zika virus, or Ebola, or in my case, motor vehicle safety. We didn't go after trying to just frame it as a public health issue. We also said it's a financial issue with huge impacts on your society. We got the World Bank involved, which validated that and therefore got other finance ministers involved.

So you find ways to broaden your stakeholder base by defining the problems in terms that are within their resources or responsibilities so they feel they can do something about it and it will make a difference.

Interviewer: That sounds like the sort of skill that gets better the more times you do it.

Ricardo Martinez: Yes, it does. You learn from others. I had a couple of great mentors. I always sought help, but one of the mentors said, "You've got to understand the "Power Pie."

I didn't quite get that concept. He made it clear, "You've got to understand the power pie before you get into something" because anybody that has a stake in the issue that you leave out will show up at the very end and will obstruct the process.

So we really had to get pretty good at understanding who the players were and make sure we brought them in.

> **"You've got to understand the "Power Pie" before you get into something because anybody you leave out will show up at the very end and obstruct the process."**
> —Dr. Ricardo Martinez

But then you also have to figure out who really has the resources and who has the capability to make a difference and how. Everyone can find a role to play.

For what it's worth, I purposely landed in the Department of Transportation because of my interest in preventing traffic injuries, and being a physician, people asked, "What the hell are you doing here?" My answer was, "I'm here because this is where the resources are."

With all due respect to my colleagues in medicine, they did a great job of documenting information on the clinical aspects of all these terrible deaths and injuries, but they didn't do much to prevent the injuries. What's worse, the people building the roads lived in another building and had a very different viewpoint of the world. People building the cars were yet another group of people with a separate view.

So I went to where the transportation leaders were. Sometimes that's what you have to do to get the right resources involved in the solution. You have to decide, okay, here's a problem, but am I really going to be able to fix it, or do I have to bring a group of people together and reframe it to their perspective in order to have the resources allocated to solve it?

Interviewer: *So you're talking about a pie—slices of a pie like a raspberry pie—but it's a Power Pie?*

Ricardo Martinez: Yes, one with all those slices that create that whole pie, just like you'd look at a pie chart. Ask yourself, "Where's the power?" Design that.

All too often you find people that leave out slivers, and those slivers may have a lot of political power or they may be very influential. If they're not involved in the process, you've got a problem. Be afraid of creating that problem.

> **"All too often you find people leave out slivers, and those slivers may have a lot of political power or they may be very influential. If they're not involved in the process, you've got a problem. Be afraid of creating that problem."**
>
> — Dr. Ricardo Martinez

Interviewer: *What process might you use to make sure you're including the right people in the power pie?*

Ricardo Martinez: Well, it's funny. We now use the word "socialize" a lot, which is probably a better term, but I just used to say, "Walk it around."

I would go out and bring the topic out to others. I often found that you're always talking to the same people, and the problem has been persisting for years.

That's really a clue that you may not have the people who have all the resources involved, so you have to ask what the issue is, who has influence, and whether they've been invited to the table. And do we have a way for them to participate?

Let me give you an example about injuries to young kids or teenagers.

Where is that group spending their time? Well, they live all day at school. So we wanted relationships with schools and started building relationships with science teachers.

We built relationships with science teachers because when you try to teach traffic safety in a school curriculum, you're competing with teen pregnancy and smoking, and those sorts of issues.

But if you're working with school science teachers, then you are teaching math, velocity, speed, acceleration, and forces, and it was really cool. So we actually found ourselves bringing in non-traditional partners.

In terms of the power pie itself, I was really kind of using that. Teachers are stakeholders in terms of the power pie when it comes to getting into the classroom. It's who has a vested or political interest and making sure that you go out and acknowledge them or talk to them.

So if we wanted to do something with child safety seats, then I should map out who has the authority and the responsibility for the state level. Who's got the federal level? What do the car manufacturers say? What do the child seat manufacturers say?

Is there anyone we're leaving out? Okay, what about law enforcement? They've got a stake in this, correct? They've got to enforce these laws.

So just make sure that as you look at your solution, or potential solutions, the people who have political influence are going to be part of the process and have a say in the development of the process.

Interviewer: *As I've had contributors talk about how to make collaboration successful, they often talk about selecting the right people to collaborate with—individuals who, for whatever reason, have some collaboration skills or they get along well with others.*

Do you think that the ability to get along with other people, and to be liked and to like others is a critical characteristic of people who will be successful in collaboration?

Ricardo Martinez: There's a great comment by Lieutenant General Russel L. Honore, the guy sent down to New Orleans by the military after things were just falling apart after Katrina. They brought him in, and he talked about teamwork.

He said that it's nice to have a happy team, but he's seen a lot of happy teams that don't do jack. [Laughs]

The bigger issue is that instead of just being nice or being liked, the real skills for collaborations are to be able to listen, to understand, and to build the relationships. People actually respect competence over niceness.

People will trust you if they think you're competent, but they'll also invest more into creating success if they think they have been heard.

That's the other thing about building a success with collaboration. It's not just about getting people to sign on to your view or vision of the world; it's really about understanding through the process what the problem really is and what the solutions might be.

That's really important because it goes back to this power pie concept. The thing that I've often found is that if you left somebody out who has a stake in the game when you began to move forward, they often went into obstructionist mode, and it wasn't always because they were evil or because they were against it; it was mostly because they didn't feel they'd been heard. This wasn't something you were doing *with* them; you were doing *to* them.

> "The thing that I've often found is that if you left somebody out who has a stake in the game, when you began to move forward, they often went into obstructionist mode . . . because they didn't feel they'd been heard.
>
> This wasn't something you were doing **with** them; you were doing **to** them."
> —Dr. Ricardo Martinez

Interviewer: You talked about good listening. What are the keys to being a good listener?

Ricardo Martinez: Well, two things: what's said and what's not said—and then being able to explore.

When you begin to meet with somebody and talk with them before trust is developed, the level of the conversation may be much more superficial than you really need to get to.

When they first start, they may speak in positions and may give their perceptions, and as you listen to them, you repeat it back to them, and you try to explore that. You will find that they will reveal more and more of their true concerns, and what you look for is common ground.

> **"You listen to them, you repeat it back to them, and you try to explore that.**
>
> **You will find that they will reveal more and more of their true concerns, and what you look for is common ground."**
>
> **—Dr. Ricardo Martinez**

Often, you'll start with your differences, but then you need to find where the common ground is. In *Getting The Yes*, the negotiations group out of Harvard talks about how people often start with their positions, but what you really want to do is to define their interest.

When you define their interest and meet their interest, their positions often disappear or are much more moveable.

And what happens is the greater the spectrum of people you can get to collaborate with, the stronger and more effective your collaboration is in the community. Having said that, you may not get everybody to go along. If I want to raise the drinking age, I'm probably not going to get a lot of support from the alcohol sellers. I'm going to go talk with them and listen to their concerns. I'm going to try to make sure that we've got a collaboration that tries not to put them in a negative position. That's all fine.

But on the other side of the coin, for them it's sales, right? They may not want to participate or even be against the effort, but at least you engaged them, and they understand the goal and the rationale.

Interviewer: *It's interesting. It seems that if I were titling the book based on what you're saying about collaboration, it would almost be, Collaboration . . . A Strategic Exercise, because a lot of your thinking about collaboration falls into the area of strategic thinking. It's not so much a touchy-feely thing or warmth with people; it's a lot of strategic considerations. Is that accurate?*

Ricardo Martinez: Absolutely. It's a necessity in order to be effective. Let me give you a good example. If you look at our agency, the Department Of Transportation, the National Highway Traffic Safety Administration accounted for less than 1% of the overall budget, but traffic crashes accounted for about 96% of all the deaths and injuries.

By far, motor vehicles were the biggest problem, so much so that people were almost accepting of those deaths and injuries. If there was a death in aviation, on the other hand, it shows up in headline news. There was the same thing with railroads and others, yet those relatively few crashes were dwarfed by the public problem of road-related death and injury.

So the question is when you've got the magnitude of the problem and the least of budget, how do you succeed? The only way you're going to be successful is to use other people's money and to allocate other people's resources. They have to be part of the solution.

The strategy wasn't going to be big government, and it wasn't going to be big money, so it had to be big change. We had to get other people to see this as an issue that they wanted to allocate their resources to. We could do that in a coordinated fashion and be more effective together. So yes, it's all about the strategy of attacking the problem in new ways.

Interviewer: *Does strategy come naturally to you?*

Ricardo Martinez: That's an interesting question. I would say that being a little bit "out of the box" probably comes from my varied experiences and perspectives over the years, and having good mentors helped me do that. But I think what we're finding is that more and more people are able to see these connections that maybe I saw earlier—getting out of the silos. I think it's easier and easier because of the amount of information available and the growth of big data, so you can quickly learn and get an understanding of what the landscape looks like faster than we've ever been able to do before.

> **"I think it's easier and easier because of the amount of information available and the growth of big data, so you can quickly learn and get an understanding of what the landscape looks like faster than we've ever been able to do before."**
> **—Dr. Ricardo Martinez**

Interviewer: *Is there anything else about collaboration you'd like to share?*

Ricardo Martinez: Yes, in terms of collaboration, you really need to have continued communications around some shared goals. And you know, collaboration is not always big initiatives. Sometimes it's about positioning yourself differently with the targets that you're trying to protect or you're trying to get engaged with.

I'll give you a good example. We were looking at a really unusual pattern of child injuries and deaths in the Texas and Arizona border cities with Mexico, which were highly Hispanic, Mexican background. The states already had child safety seat laws, yet we had a high percentage of deaths of children—infants really—overrepresented in that area.

So we said, "Okay, you're not going to solve this problem from Washington, DC, and it's not going to be solved from the top." We needed to go to the local communities and say, "Here is the data. We want you to see your problem. This is affecting your children, and we've got all these tools you can use to prevent your children from being injured. We'll help you."

In other words, you position yourself as being a supporter—a resource to people who are activated about their community, their own families, and friends.

So a really fascinating thing happened. You'll love this story. It turns out these children were being carried in the laps of the mothers in the front seat of the car.

There was an empty child seat in the back because state law required child seats. The parents owned the child seats, but the kids were not being put in them.

The moms were holding them, and when a crash would occur, the child would be killed or be seriously injured either from the airbag, being crushed by mom moving forward in the crash, or because the mom couldn't hold the child and the child would fly in the air.

And so that was a real head-scratcher. How did that happen?

From continued conversation with the community at risk, we learned that it was the mothers-in-law who told the children's mothers, "Hey, you married my son, and when he was a baby, I carried him in my lap to protect him. Now you're telling me that you're going to put the child in the backseat. That means you don't want or love my grandchild."

So the mothers would feel kind of intimidated and would take the child out of the child seat so the child would be loved like grandma insisted, right? What was the solution? The solution was that the local communities got together and designated days when the priests would bless the seats. They have these great photographs of these moms with these child seats and candles, and the priest is blessing the seats.

So basically, this solution came out of the community. This was an innovation that came from the community trying to solve their problem through their culture in their way.

Once the priests blessed the child seats, the moms could put the children back in the child seats, and after that trumped the mother-in-law, we saw a significant decrease in the number of injuries to kids in that area.

That was a collaboration where our approach was: "This is your problem. We've got the data for you. We want you to be successful. How can we help? Here are some of the solutions."

And then the local community said, "Okay, how do we get from here to the solution of putting the kids in the back seat?" They figured out what their barriers were within their own culture, and then they figured out the way to overcome the cultural issues.

> **"They figured out what their barriers were within their own culture, and then they figured out the way to overcome the cultural issues."**
> —Dr. Ricardo Martinez

It's fascinating, just fascinating.

Interviewer: Well, that's the kind of thing that can't happen if you're not listening.

Ricardo Martinez: Without a doubt. There are a couple of approaches, right? One of them was to be authoritative: "Hey, you've got a child seat law. Put the kid in it and in the back seat."

Another approach was, "You've got a law, and you must put the kid in the back. You do this, or you're a bad mother—or be arrested." Right?

The other one was, "These are your kids, and we're concerned, and we want to work with you to help you solve it." They were horrified when they saw the injury numbers for children being overrepresented in their community.

So then their question shifted to, "What are we going to do about it?"

We said, "We don't know what's causing it," so they had to figure that out. And we kind of taught them some ways to do that.

That's the other thing about our collaboration. It is about teaching people how to fish, how to do it, and let them be innovative and come up with the solutions.

Interviewer: *I would imagine that a committee, given three months, would never guess that that was going to be the issue. I mean, I can see a lot of guesses coming along, but the mother-in-law?*

Ricardo Martinez: You really should see the photographs; it's fascinating. I actually remember that "aha moment" well because I was sitting at my desk in Washington, and people came into my office and gave me the presentation. I had to see for myself. I traveled constantly to get to the communities and had been down to El Paso several times with my dad, who taught there.

I visited the collaboration, and the one I joined was at a Jewish-owned auto parts store with a large parking lot. On Sundays after Catholic Church, the Hispanic dads would go over there since the auto parts store was open on Sunday. They would drive over, buy parts, and work on their cars in the parking lot. While they worked on their cars, the moms would bring all the child seats, and the priest who had finished morning church would go over there and bless all those seats placed in a semi-circle. It was lovely.

So it was like a win-win. The auto shop loved it, the dads loved it, the mom's loved it, and it made a difference. It usually occurred on Sunday afternoons when the priest was available.

It was just phenomenal. It was a bottoms-up approach, though we started it top-down.

> **"Child safety seat use . . . It was a bottoms-up approach, though we started it top-down."**
>
> —Dr. Ricardo Martinez

Interviewer: *The interesting part of the story is that a lot of safety professionals and medical experts might not look at religion as a solution to a societal problem, but in this case, it was.*

People think that solutions are going to be within the systems where they live.

Ricardo Martinez: I raised that particular one because I'm reviewing an article for somebody, and they really talk about how public health's got to be in charge and public health needs to do this and that. I think public health is outgunned and outmanned, so the real question is how do you effectively leverage your resources? Being in charge doesn't always mean being successful.

A big challenge is that you're going to have to bring a lot of players to the issue. How does one do it strategically? Sure, you can position yourself as being in charge and asking them to support you. Good luck with that.

But the other approach that is really effective within a single community, group, or culture is by engaging them in a non-confrontational style, where you are positioning yourself as a trusted advisor having the same concerns they do. They have to be the ones activated to implement, and you've got some resources and tools to help them.

I found the same thing with the black community. That community was worried about social justice. They didn't generally focus on traffic safety as a pressing concern, so we went to the National Conference of Black Churches, shared the data and the impact of traffic injuries and deaths on their culture, and they came up with the movie *Heaven Can Wait* as one of their programs. I learned a lot from them.

The bottom line is that in terms of being effective, we are beginning to understand more and more how connected things are, so to be effective, you have to create those connections.

And it has to be around a shared vision and goals. Being engaged in an issue is optional. People are discretionary; they have to commit to doing something because it's good for them and they believe in it.

So that's really the idea of being able to provide that leadership—to be able to be trusted, to be able to make an initiative seen as something that makes a difference, and to be able to do it. Those are the key aspects to that.

Interviewer: *I think your story is fascinating because it takes a lot of wisdom to hear an out-of-the-box solution like involving priests to bless child safety seats, which frankly is not part of allopathic medicine, and to recognize that as a legitimate solution.*

And you have to be flexible in your thinking to realize that the solution could be completely outside your experience. In the last 500 years, there's been some separation between the approach to medicine and the church, yet in this case, they had to come together to make it work.

Ricardo Martinez: Quite frankly, that's actually happening right now with another client out West, where they're beginning to get the church involved a little bit more because they have such an influence on people, especially in the target culture. I think that you're going to see more and more of that, and it's really such an opportunity for public health—looking for those natural affinities and alignment, and bringing people around an issue so that it's framed within their culture. It requires changing the approach from these things we try to attack in isolation. That is not nearly as effective.

BETTY BEKEMEIER, PhD, MPH, RN

Betty Bekemeier is associate professor at the University of Washington School of Nursing and director of the UW School of Public Health's Northwest Center for Public Health Practice. She is a distinguished public health systems researcher and has worked extensively toward improving the effectiveness of our prevention systems and related workforce. She has led numerous studies regarding local health department services and their impact on health outcomes and health disparities. Dr. Bekemeier is a primary investigator of the Public Health Activities and Services Tracking (PHAST) study initiated through the Robert Wood Johnson Foundation Nurse Faculty Scholars Program.

Interviewer: You are unique in that you go back and forth from academia to practice. It's like you're one of those ancient organisms that can live in both an aquatic and land environment! That has to take some collaborative skills. How you would define collaboration?

Betty Bekemeier: I go back to years ago, when I worked as part of a group of leaders. I helped staff and lead this group that developed a curriculum around collaborative leadership. That was in connection with The Turning Point National Initiative, which was funded by the Robert Wood Johnson Foundation. We worked with 21 states around the country, and our office led this initiative. I was deputy director under Bobbie Berkowitz, who was director.

It was about a 10-year project, and I was deputy in the last five years or so. It was really all about supporting the development of radical kinds of systems change—public health systems changes in these 21 states—and something that bubbled up a lot was the importance of collaborative leadership and generating a culture of collaborative leadership to really make things happen.

In that spirit, we had the opportunity to develop this collaborative leadership curriculum. If you go to collaborativeleadership.org, it's still there. It's a static website that's sat there for a long time now, but people still use that curriculum, and I occasionally get requests to do workshops around that. I don't do them anymore, but I have former Turning Point colleagues who do.

I hearken back to some of that around some of the real key collaborative leadership principles, and the one that really comes to mind is building and maintaining trust.

To me, that is just so critical, and a lot of that for me boils down to things like following up on what you say you're going to do and recognizing you're not the expert.

Yes, I bring expertise, and I bring that to the table, but really honoring and recognizing the expertise that others bring is another big piece—and genuinely honoring that expertise.

If people don't feel it or think it's genuine, you don't get anywhere.

> **"Really honoring and recognizing the expertise that others bring is another big piece . . . If people don't feel it or think it's genuine, you don't get anywhere."**
> —Dr. Betty Bekemeier

So it has to be that way. I think those are the things that kind of bubble up to the top for me about establishing and maintaining trust. When that trust is ever challenged or undermined in some way, that means getting on the phone and talking about it—having crucial conversations.

Interviewer: *Do you have a story that shows that someone in the collaboration felt the respect wasn't genuine and the trust was off-track?*

Betty Bekemeier: It seems I've done a fair amount of cleaning up behind other people who don't necessarily exemplify this. And maybe there's someone who has had to clean up after me from time to time too!

Interviewer: *You have a big truck with brushes on the back that squirts water like a street-cleaner?*

Betty Bekemeier: There are many times when I'm working on a project with a group, and I am on this fence between academia and practice. I say, technically, my butt is in the ivory tower, but I rest my feet in public health practice. And it takes a lot of time, a lot of energy, and a lot of weekends to sort of maintain that. Because a lot of these are friendships too, friendships that you have to have in both places, right?

Most of my collaborations in my area are doing a lot of work with a lot of state and local public health practice people who are really stretched and have a lot of challenges, and I see my job as advancing their work, as helping generate the evidence they need for decision making. That's what I do for my research. And being responsive to their workforce development and leadership development needs is part of my job as director of the Northwest Center For Public Health Practice.

So there are a lot of times when I ask them for things. I'm working on a project with them, and I say, "Hey, you've got to write this great work of yours up. We've got to get this out so other people will know about this research we did together or this project you guys did that's so amazing."

And so, I might be able to advance their important work by helping take the leadership on moving along the publication of their work. We then may have deadlines. I'm writing this stuff up or working with them to do so, and I'm asking them to respond and give me information, or I'm asking for them to review this or weigh in on that.

But they have everyday work to do, and emergencies to respond to, and here I am, this kind of academic, asking them to . . .

Interviewer: *Do more stuff.*

Betty Bekemeier: And it's stuff that's not part of their job description, typically. So when I do that, I'm really careful. I had an experience about a month ago or so when I was talking with a bunch of people about something we were working on. One of them piped up and said, "Betty, I'll do it, because every time I do something for you I get it back five times over."

That was so gratifying to me because on the one hand, it sort of exemplifies how much work this is because you have to overdeliver to be a good partner. But it was also great to hear that from him—that level of appreciation and recognition and awareness—that I do try to overdeliver. And so that's a big part of this too, you know. I'm asking for their amazing expertise.

Interviewer: *Do they do it—participate—because they believe in the concept of efficacy?*

Betty Bekemeier: Yes, because the other thing I always try to do is to have a mission— a shared mission and a shared vision. I guess that's another kind of principle, right? And if I stay close with my colleagues, and I know what they're struggling with, what their needs are, what I can deliver on, and what my expertise can bring, then if they've got the long view, they see I can support their practice.

Leading a research study, a practice-based research study with them, doesn't generate change overnight, right? It takes a long time, and they're not going to see anything overnight, but when they have a long enough view and see me as having a shared vision with them to help them advance a practice, then I would like to think that says a lot.

But that means I need to have my ear to the ground and know what their issues are. I have to overdeliver when I ask for things. I need to really be respectful of their expertise, or I'll not get anywhere.

When I do something at the last minute because I got behind or because I missed something, and I ask my buddies to respond more quickly than I think they can, or should, or need to, I apologize.

Some of my closest colleagues say I apologize too much, but I think apology, sincere apology, goes a long way.

> **"When I do something at the last minute . . . and ask my buddies to respond more quickly than I think they can . . . I apologize.**
>
> **I think apology, sincere apology, goes a long way."**
>
> —Dr. Betty Bekemeier

Those that don't apologize might be more successful in some ways, but those that do, I think, are more successful collaboratively.

There is a leadership guru, Jim Collins, who wrote *Good To Great*. He has done a lot of research on leadership, and the real take-away for me from his books is that you don't actually know the names of the really successful leaders who have moved forward out of challenging times [in companies], and the improvements are sustained over time. They don't generally become famous.

We tend not to know their names because as Jim Collins says, "They put the right people in the right seats on the bus," and also, by the way, get the wrong people off the bus.

On my research team we always talk about the bus—and our bus. Sometimes people, even nationally, will say, "Can I join your bus? You guys have so much fun and do such good stuff, we want on the bus too."

At the end of my presentations, I'll often talk about our bus and have a little picture of a bus. It's my way of saying, "It's not just me." It's a real collaborative effort of a whole bunch of people with really great expertise that they all bring to play.

Interviewer: The image of the bus is wonderful because all ideas are communicated more effectively with an image. And a bus says you're together, and you're moving forward in a positive direction—under control, with wise *leadership, and in many ways making the whole thing more comfortable. If I put a picture of apple pie on a menu, the food starts to look better already. It's a nice image.*

Another thought. Collaboration takes time—time—time. It takes time to accomplish something through a collaborative effort, likely much more time than it would take to do it on your own. It takes time to work with each person, and many people may be on the bus. Can you speak to the time warp of collaboration?

Betty Bekemeier: Yes. And that can be really hard.

It takes a lot of time up front. That time becomes less once you've established patterns of trust and experience with one another.

I don't have to explain myself with my practice partners. There are times when I will ask for permission to talk about these data or present this at this national meeting, but it's so-and-so's data that we've done thus-and-so with, and I'll ask permission and the person will say, "It's okay, Betty; just run with it."

My point is that they trust that I'm not going to make them look bad and that I will handle their data or their information in a respectful way, and it will advance our mutual cause or vision and not undermine them.

So I don't always have to explain. I err on the side of caution, so I send them an email, but there's no cleanup involved afterwards. It takes less time.

I've also been involved with organizations in which I had a lot of responsibility and collaborative leadership hadn't been the norm.

And you're right. It takes an inordinate amount of time to figure out how to effectively shift the culture because I cannot operate any other way.

It means a certain amount of reorganization, of trust building, of allowing for risk. It means that you give people a lot more responsibility than they've had before, and some mistakes can occur, but we learn from those mistakes. So be it. And it takes time.

> "Some mistakes can occur when you give others more responsibility, but we learn from those mistakes. So be it."
> —Dr. Betty Bekemeier

So how do I manage that?

For one thing, I work a lot. I work too much all the time, so it runs into my life, but these are all relationships that I enjoy and that are important to me, so that's not so bad.

Interviewer: There are a couple of themes that I heard you talk about that I'd like you to comment on.

First, it sounds like you're saying that, yes, there is a lot of time involved in collaboration, but if you already have a preexisting level of genuine trust, you can reduce some of that time.

So it's not like starting over again each time. Once you have that trust built, collaboration can be faster, reducing the time warp.

Betty Bekemeier: Yes.

Interviewer: You used the word "enjoy" when talking about collaborative efforts. Could you speak a bit about the importance of enjoying working with other people?

Betty Bekemeier: The need to enjoy—well for one thing, it makes the work doable. I wouldn't be able to do it without the enjoyment of it and these relationships.

If we all enjoy those relationships too, that, to me, is where I get a lot of my satisfaction. There is job satisfaction, as well as positive feedback for your efforts, when this fellow says, "Betty, we'll do anything you want because we know we get this back, and you're so great to work with." That makes it worthwhile.

I guess I'm by nature an optimist. These are folks working in very difficult and sometimes dire situations, so bringing a certain amount of joy and vision, and the feeling that we're in this together, and we're working on it together, help give voice to that and support for change.

Interviewer: *I don't know that you could put the hours in you do if you didn't enjoy working with people. Working 35 hours a week is one thing; working 70 hours in a week is another. When you put so many hours in working with people, it almost becomes a part of your social existence. Or perhaps it's a dual reality of work and social experience.*

Betty Bekemeier: Right. In my position, too, I feel a certain obligation if I have access to information and data that others don't to not make myself out to be the expert but to make sure that data is part of the mix. It's rewarding and fun at the same time.

PAUL C. ERWIN, MD, DrPH

Dr. Paul Erwin is professor and head of the department of public health, University of Tennessee. Having worked as regional director and health officer for the Tennessee Department of Health for 16 years, Dr. Erwin has expertise in public health practice, community-based public health systems, and services research. He was a member of the NACCHO Work Group that developed Mobilizing for Action through Planning and Partnerships (MAPP) and later served as chair of the work group during the early years of implementation. He has published articles describing academic-practice engagement via MAPP as well as an article summarizing methods in data synthesis to identify strategic issues.

Interviewer: Much of your career has focused on what we can accurately call collaborative efforts in public health. What have you learned from years of experience?

Paul Erwin: What matters is attitude and perceptions, because there are numerous opportunities to collaborate, and I think having an open and inviting attitude essentially says, "We don't have all the answers; I don't have all the answers. Whatever this thing is that we're dealing with is larger than any one of us can address, and encouraging that kind of openness and interest in other people's perspectives and opinions is crucial."

It's actually both an attitude and a philosophy. That's my overarching sense of what makes collaborations possible.

Interviewer: Do you feel that collaboration can be intimidating for someone attempting it for the first time?

Paul Erwin: I guess it can be. For people who have little experience with community partners, municipal organizations, or people who don't have or wear the same stripes as they do, I'm sure it might be anxiety provoking. It's new ground, and in that sense, anytime any of us does anything new, there may be some anxiety. The hope is that with the right kinds of mentorship and guidance, there would be less trepidation, less concern about uncharted waters, so to speak.

Interviewer: If you were speaking to a class made up of students getting their masters in public health, and you were introducing them to the concept of the collaboration process, what would you say?

Paul Erwin: Again, I think I would lead off with the same kinds of comments that I made about attitude and philosophy. I do think it takes a certain degree of willingness and capability to be humble and flexible. I would say to the students, and I do say to students—especially in our field of public health, which is multi-disciplinary from the get-go—one cannot accomplish things in this field without collaboration. It's an essential element in public health practice, and I would extend that to say it becomes an essential element to academic public health settings as well. That's part of what I've been trying to promote in our university setting.

> **"I do think it takes a certain degree of willingness and capability to be humble and to be flexible. One cannot accomplish things in this field without collaboration."**
> —Dr. Paul C. Erwin

Paul Erwin: Public health issues arise in such a multi-disciplinary context. Think about the social determinants of health, for example. So if public health issues originate in such contexts, it stands to reason that in order for us to successfully address these, we must take a multi-disciplinary approach. And in the practice setting, that can only come about through collaboration.

Interviewer: Are there situations, based on their nature, that don't appear to you as a good fit for collaboration? People might look at a scenario and say, "I don't think this collaboration has a chance."

Paul Erwin: For collaboration to be successful, all partners must be able to envision mutual benefit. You either need to completely retool or step away from those collaborations that become a one-way street.

Interviewer: Do you have a story of collaboration you feel represents the best collaboration has to offer?

Paul Erwin: I do, and I've written a little bit about it. If you probe deeply in my CV, you may eventually come across it. When I was with the Tennessee Department of Health, before being in my current position in academia, we were engaged with local communities in facilitating community-based health assessment and planning processes. The groups with whom we worked on the local level were county health councils. Those health councils were made up of leaders and movers and shakers in these small rural communities, as well as grass roots people—people who were interested in, and concerned about, health and health care.

After examining lots of secondary data and collecting some primary data, we noted that Scott County had the highest lung cancer death rates and the highest heart disease death rates in the state, as well as other severe issues with mental health and substance abuse. However, when it came to prioritizing issues, the health council in Scott County concluded that the number one priority was dental health for their children. There was not a single provider in the entire county who was willing to see children on Medicaid. The children had to go out of county to be seen for both routine and restorative dental care. The health council members described their situation in very clear language: "We see our children in pain and discomfort in school, and when they're suffering in school, they can't concentrate; and when they can't concentrate, they don't do well; and when they don't do well, they flunk; and when they flunk, they drop out; and when they drop out, they can't get a good job; and when they can't get a good job, they don't have health insurance; and then when their children grow up, they can't get their children dental care either." This is the vicious cycle of poverty and poor health.

From our Tennessee Department of Health perspective, we could have responded, "Dental health or dental issues don't kill a lot of people in Scott County; smoking does, not wearing seatbelts does, substance abuse does." But I think we recognized that from a collaborative perspective, had we weighed in heavily with that, we would have lost the health council.

The issue of oral health was real; it was palpable; and it was one where there was a lot of energy and a lot of interest generated locally. So our role in that was to facilitate what they wished us to do about this, which ultimately resulted in the establishment of a rural pediatric dental facility—as fine a one as you can find anywhere.

And with the success of that, the health council was then prepared to take that same energy and that same level of concern on "upstream" approaches to improving oral health, including reducing sugar-sweetened beverages and the appropriate use of fluoride. Then they were more open and eager to move on to larger issues such as heart disease and lung cancer, and to address those issues at the community level.

I think that it is important to recognize that one can set the collaborative up for failure, if you try to steer it in a way that goes against where the energy is heading, and that one has to bring to a collaborative a great degree of patience and willingness to think differently about levels of perspective you may not have.

Interviewer: *Is there anything else on collaboration you'd like to share?*

Paul Erwin: One of the great challenges that we constantly see has to do with sustainability of collaboration, because often, at the outset of a collaborative venture, there's a lot of energy. A lot of people want to get involved, participate, and be a part, yet invariably you find over time in most of these situations that interest begins to wane.

How do you find the right kinds of success and levels of achievement or engagement that sustains collaboration—at least sustains it to the point to give it an opportunity for success?

Most collaboratives in public health need to have a long timeframe. We rarely move the needle overnight. There are a few things that can have quick turnarounds, but those are less common.

In thinking about collaboratives that we've been able to maintain, part of the key was being able to institutionalize the collaborative. By that I mean to formalize it in a way that it moves the collaborative beyond just the individuals who might have initiated it.

Because people move on, and when people go, where's the institutional memory and wherewithal to continue what has been a good collaborative?

The best example of this for us is our Academic Health Department collaborative between our academic department [at the University of Tennessee, Knoxville] and the Knox County Health Department. Although there had been successful collaborations over many years, we recognized the need to formalize the collaboration in a way that would better ensure mutual benefits related to teaching, practice-based research, and service for academic faculty, students, and public health practitioners. When the current leaders move on, this collaborative will remain in place because of that formal structure.

Interviewer: Thank you for bringing up the significance of the sustainability of the collaborative.

GAIL REED, MS

Gail Reed is founding director of Medical Education Cooperation with Cuba (MEDICC), a US nonprofit that for 20 years has promoted cooperation among the US, Cuban, and global health communities to improve health and health equity worldwide, including the USA. She is MEDICC's executive editor of the peer-reviewed journal *MEDICC Review*, publishing work by developing-country health professionals. Reed produced *¡Salud!*, winner of the Council on Foundation's Henry Hampton Award for Excellence in Film; delivered a TEDMED talk ("Where to train the world's doctors? Cuba"); and authored a 300-page study on the impact of the US embargo on health in Cuba.

Interviewer: *Could you share some of your thoughts on collaboration?*

Gail Reed: My primary experience has been collaborating with the health system and professionals of a country whose government hasn't been recognized by the United States for decades: Cuba. Luckily, that situation is rapidly evolving. The other part of my experience has been with organizations and foundations in the States, working together around health issues and global health cooperation.

The first piece of advice to people and organizations seeking to work with others would be: leave your baggage at home. When you're talking with a new contact, whether it is in the United States or abroad in health or fundraising, or whatever field, try to leave behind your baggage, your assumptions, and preconceived notions. Listen with an open mind because you're going to find out a lot of things that surprise you and that are going to be essential to move any kind of collaboration forward.

> **"When you're talking with a new contact . . . leave behind your baggage, your assumptions, and preconceived notions."**
> —Gail Reed

Interviewer: Can you give a lively example of "leaving your baggage at home"? It sounds like a great idea.

Gail Reed: I am, in many ways, a child of the sixties. I first went to Cuba in the 1960s, after the Cuban revolution of 1959, with a large group of students. When we first came together before travelling to Cuba, a lot of the white women were braless and very hippie looking, and the African American women were in Afros, carrying them with lots of pride. Certainly, none of us wore nail polish.

Then we got to Cuba, where we met women who had actually participated in that revolutionary process. But the darker-skinned Cuban women had their hair straightened, the lighter-skinned women were wearing rollers in their hair, and all of them were wearing bright nail polish. They didn't conform at all to our "standards" of what they should look like as builders of a new, different kind of society. In short, we thought they needed to look like us because ours was *the* way, and we were confident ours *was the* wave of the future.

It threw us for a loop; we had to rethink, and that was just a superficial moment of what was different about Cuba. We couldn't make all of these assumptions, and the idea of not taking your baggage is really not to take all of your assumptions into a conversation, especially a first conversation.

You'll then be much more sensitive to nuance; you'll be more sensitive to where other people are coming from—their own experience and what has led them to the table with you—and it's not always the reasons you think.

Interviewer: *What are various ways to craft questions to start conversations in this early phase you're describing that would reflect the philosophy you're presenting? Telling somebody to put your baggage aside is almost like "Don't be you." That's not so easy.*

Gail Reed: Just to go back a bit, leaving your baggage behind doesn't mean "not being you." It simply means it's fine to be you, but it also means to listen—listen, and listen hard—to open your mind a bit in order to do that, and leave behind that part of you that has all these presumptions.

The other thing is I don't think there are any instant "conversation starters" because the first thing you have to do is your homework—whether it's a funder, another organization, or someone from another country. You need to find out as much as you can about the person who's going to be sitting across from you or the audience that's going to be in front of you.

Perhaps this seems contradictory to leaving your baggage at home, but I don't think so. Finding out as much as you can about the person you're going to meet will give you some clue as to what you have in common, where you might look for those magic points of intersection and agreement. And those, after all, are the starting points for a relationship.

You might be looking ahead strategically to build trust over time, or to do something more urgent or concrete together in the short run, or just to open a dialogue to be continued.

If you're sitting with a foundation, and you know that they're not particularly interested in global health, but they're very interested in helping improve health in vulnerable communities in the United States, then in my case, I would be looking at what Cuba does that could be relevant to that goal. What about prevention? What about chronic diseases? What are the main programs that this organization or foundation has that the experience in Cuba, however different, might be seen as value-added for them. And then these foundation representatives might look at my non-governmental organization or me differently. They might leave some of their own baggage behind that had pegged my work as unrelated to their mission of improving health at home.

Interviewer: You are illuminating a critical idea: to find and identify that area of common interest. From your experience, is it obvious how both organizations might benefit?

Gail Reed: It's not obvious at all—because no matter what is on any website or what is on your website, you're not telling the whole story of what is of interest to you, your foundation, institution, or organization.

You've got your public message out there, but what's behind it could be quite different, representing more current thinking. Maybe your board is considering a whole new direction. Maybe you're engaging in a new project area or initiative, and that's not going to be immediately apparent—even to the person who does their homework about you.

So I think you have to ferret out the areas of mutual interest in different ways. Listening is so important because they're going to tell you about themselves, and you're going to tell them about yourself. In my experience, if you're the one who asked for the meeting, try to do the listening first, because what they say will help guide you when it's your turn to talk. Listening will help you pick out what you want to say about yourself or your work that is most likely to strike a chord, to resonate with your new acquaintance.

It's also a sign of respect that you want to listen to them first.

> **"Try to do the listening first, because what they say will help guide you when it's your turn to talk."**
> —Gail Reed

Things are not always apparent. They might be if you've done your homework, but they might not be. That's another reason to leave a bit of your baggage behind. You always thought this organization was about such-and-such, but maybe they're moving in different direction.

I was in a meeting recently in Washington with a lot of the unusual suspects around collaboration with Cuba, and at the table were people that I never thought I would be sitting with.

There were pharmaceutical companies, elevator companies, senators, and the former head of homeland security, and we were all talking about collaboration, and I said, "I think we need a working group on such-and-such."

One woman looked at me and said, "You're absolutely right; let's do it."

And so all of a sudden, I found myself in this situation where I had said something that resonated with her, and it wasn't because it was on her institution's website.

This is another key thing: what is that old saying attributed to Native Americans? "The success of a rain dance is in large part due to the timing." You also have to deal with issues of timing. Maybe a year ago, we would not even have sat at the same table.

> **"You also have to deal with issues of timing."**
> —Gail Reed

You also have to play catch-up fast sometimes—"Oh, I wasn't expecting this." Then you have to listen doubly hard because these are people who may be ahead of their institutions in many ways. They're ahead of the game; they're looking for the new opportunities.

They're the leaders, and so when you engage with a leader, it's different than engaging with a program director. When you're engaging with leaders, they are the vision—they're the ones who are developing that vision, so you need to play catch up very fast.

> **"When you engage with a leader, it's different than engaging with a program director. They are the vision . . . so you need to play catch up very fast."**
> —Gail Reed

Interviewer: You've been answering the question, "How do you find things that are in common?"

Gail Reed: Points in common also means that without losing your own essential mission, you're willing to be a bit flexible about how that is messaged and how that might relate to someone else.

For example, we [MEDICC] just got a grant from a major foundation that doesn't do international health, so a lot of the messaging to them—and on their website about their program with us—has to do with how the program intersects with and improves US health, or health status or collaboration in the US towards health, and doesn't have so much to do with Cuba, except on the back end.

Our message about Cuba is on the front end, but that doesn't really matter because essentially where we come together is around the search for innovation that leads us to health equity. That leads us to a healthier society, and of course, universal health care. That's our point of contact. Where we start from in our messaging may be different, and I think we have to be a little bit flexible in understanding that.

Interviewer: *In the world of literature, we have comedies, dramas, and tragedies. If I were looking for the tragic story line in the world of collaboration, it's the situation where a collaboration is created and quickly falls flat. What advice do you have for people to be able to identify which collaborations are likely to fall apart and which will be sustainable? Can you tell me how to avoid the tragedy of failed collaborations?*

Gail Reed: There are lots of metaphors and quotes we refer to at MEDICC: one is a paraphrased quote from Albert Einstein, who said, "Life is like riding a bicycle. You have to keep moving or you'll fall off." So you continually have to look at ways in which your vision is developing and ways that other organization's—countries', whoever's—vision is developing to keep a partnership working.

Some other things apply. A wonderful representative of UNICEF that was a dear friend of mine, now departed, said, "Getting into a collaborative relationship is like wooing a lover." I'd have to say staying in is like making a marriage work; it's constant attention to relationship building. You can't assume that it´s going to go off and live happily ever after. It's not.

> **"Getting into a collaborative relationship is like wooing a lover … staying in is like making a marriage work."**
> —Gail Reed

So as not to grow apart, you need to be a) aware, and b) constantly focusing on building that relationship.

I would also say, prioritizing is important. Coming from work in a small organization, you can't build relationships with everybody you meet and would like to, so you have to also be mission-driven and see where you can add value or where they can add value to your work. It goes both ways.

But you do need to prioritize because relationship building is a very labor-intensive exercise. It takes many cups of coffee—in our case, maybe it takes a few mojitos. The best example I can give is it takes a lot of writing on the napkin together.

> **"Relationship building is a very labor-intensive exercise. It takes many cups of coffee . . . It takes a lot of writing on the napkin together."**
> —Gail Reed

"What would you do if we could do this? How do you feel about this? Things are changing, especially in our neck of the woods. Do you think such-and-such would be possible now?"

Get on the phone; get out the napkin. Begin to dream with your counterpart. That is critical because people feel the most *alive* when they're dreaming.

And if you can engage them to dream with you and vice-versa, they engage you. Then you've got a partnership that has a much longer life ahead because you're dreaming together.

Even if a project doesn't work out, that isn't the real point. The project might not work out, but your relationship will stay intact, and that's the key thing.

> **"Begin to dream with your counterpart. Even if a project does not work out . . . your relationship will stay intact, and that's the key thing."**
> —Gail Reed

Interviewer: *Those are very prescient observations. What's the big difference between collaborating with two different countries and collaborating with somebody you can go have some coffee with?*

Gail Reed: There isn't any. You have to find the people in the country you can have the coffee with. There's no difference at all.

Interviewer: *Do you have to go have coffee with them in Cuba? Do you have to go see them?*

Gail Reed: Absolutely. It's exactly the same thing. I would also say there are always issues of building trust. And some of those are more important, especially if you're working in a new environment where you're possibly not so well known.

This was the case for us in Cuba. You might also be in an environment that's been laden with prejudice or negativity, as in the case in Cuba.

Building trust is another big issue for collaborations. And that means lots and lots of transparency. What am I about? Here it is. You get what you see. You don't have hidden agendas, and if you have an agenda that goes beyond what you're saying at the table, you say so.

"This is part of a larger thing that we're working on. This is where we really want to end up, but we want your help and see if we can take some baby steps."

> **"Building trust is another big issue for collaborations. And that means lots and lots of transparency . . . If you have an agenda that goes beyond what you're saying at the table, you say so.**
> —Gail Reed

Obviously, other kinds of transparency are also important—financial transparency and all of that.

It's important that your partners—wherever they are, in the States, or abroad, or even your closest collaborators that you've worked with for years—never get blindsided by you. They get a heads up if you're going to take a new direction.

> **"It's important that your partners . . . never get blindsided by you. They get a heads up if you're going to take a new direction."**
> —Gail Reed

If you're going to sort of go off the path that the other organization, institution, or country thinks that you're on—if you're moving somewhere—give them a heads up. That's part of transparency, part of trust building, but if they get blindsided, that's a tragedy.

Interviewer: *Is there anything else you'd like to add?*

Gail Reed: One last thing I would say is don't be afraid to let your passion show. Passion is a very important part of convincing. That's a piece of advice I got very early on, and it has served me very well. Listen, yes; leave your baggage behind. But once you get to talk, don't be afraid to let your passion show.

> **"Don't be afraid to let your passion show. Passion is a very important part of convincing."**
> —Gail Reed

VIRGINIA CAINE, MD

Virginia A. Caine, MD, is an associate professor of medicine for the Infectious Disease Division of the Indiana University School of Medicine. She is the director of the Marion County Health Department and is active in several professional medical societies. She is a past president of the American Public Health Association, the nation's oldest and largest public health organization.

Interviewer: *If you were giving a talk to a grouping of masters level students, and your topic was collaboration, what would you talk about?*

Virginia Caine: What I want to tell you is, when people are really collaborating, it's sort of a dynamic process. You've got individuals, or you've got different organizations, and they all come with different perspectives, where they're working to try to solve some kind of complex problem, or there's some critical issue that they know cannot be addressed by a single individual or a single organization.

It involves a lot of people, or key stakeholders, to make a decision.

Basically, it's a process, where people or organizations work together to realize a shared goal.

> **"Collaboration is a process where people or organizations work together to realize a shared goal."**
> —Dr. Virginia Caine

And here's the other piece I think that happens a lot, and a lot of people don't realize it.

When you have this collaboration, and you're having these different people working together to solve some complex problem or critical issue where they feel that a single person can't address it, each of these individuals that come to this collaboration has their own assumptions, they have their own values, and they have their own expectations.

> **"Individuals coming to a collaboration have their own assumptions, they have their own values, and they have their own expectations."**
> —Dr. Virginia Caine

So each of them may be coming to the table based on what they think their level of expertise is, whatever skill sets they may bring to table, or any experiences that they have, and they may have certain values. So what happens is, you have this process where people are trying to flesh out together, "What's our shared vision here? What's our shared goal to try to address this complex problem, or process that we want to finish?"

And then, I don't know about other people, but most of the collaborations that I've been involved with, there always seems to be some conflict.

Conflict I think can be a good thing, because people a lot of time are more honest, you know, about what they feel and what their beliefs are.

There are people who don't even know what they don't know, trying to make decisions.

> **"Conflict I think can be a good thing, because a lot of times people are more honest, you know, about what they feel and what their beliefs are."**
> —Dr. Virginia Caine

Let's just say I'm swimming in some lake for the first time. I've never swum in it before. I'm in Florida, and I may not realize there are crocodiles or alligators in that water.

And so, you know, we're navigating this path, making an intervention, or doing something that can sometimes be dangerous, because of my lack of knowledge.

Interviewer: *You said that when you're in a group and you're trying to come up with a group vision, there can be dangers that somebody doesn't see because they're not experienced enough. You mentioned there can be conflict, but that conflict can be good.*

Do you have any recommendations for people to get through the process of creating a shared vision?

Virginia Caine: I think the thing you've got to recognize is that there is a difference sometimes in terms of the language culture, and you've gotta have effective communication.

And I may not know that I'm insulting someone. That happened to me, where I got embarrassed. We ranked #1 in the country for syphilis, and we found out that about nearly 70% of the cases were driven by illicit drug use, or some prostitution, too, but primarily it was drug use.

So I had my health department do this campaign, because you know we had to reach the drug users to come in to seek and get help. We had to address their drug addition, but we also had to test them for syphilis. And we couldn't get them to come in.

I mean they just would not come, so we finally had to reach out for some expertise. CDC sent us a person who had a lot of experience, a researcher from Columbia University who had helped to do the evaluation from a big outbreak in Harlem in New York.

And she said, "Hey, have you done a focus group with the folks you're trying to reach?"

I said, "Well, no."

And she said, "Well you know, if you really want to try to change their behavior, impact them, I think you really need to talk to the people you're trying to change."

So we interviewed some folks. You know what they told me? They told me that our campaign was very insulting, they felt it was disrespectful, and basically hell would freeze over before they came to try to get some help. And that's all because, I'm up here trying to do a process, but I didn't involve the necessary people that are part of a collaboration, that are really needed to have some impact.

They're really one of the most critical groups I needed to impact, but I didn't invite them.

And the reason we don't invite them sometimes to participate, you know, is that we feel more comfortable if we are interacting with someone that's just like us, talks like us - we're more comfortable with that type of person.

So a lot of times, when you have a collaboration, you invite the people that you know and you're comfortable with. You're not always looking for diversity in these collaboration processes.

And so, if you get like-minded people that think the same way as you, and there's no diversity in their perspective or their thoughts, you're never going to come up with any innovative solutions. You're just going to get the old, traditional, routine interventions where, wow, you may not be getting the outcomes you wanted to see.

> "We feel more comfortable if we are interacting with someone that's just like us, talks like us.
>
> If you get like-minded people thinking the same way as you, and there is no diversity in their perspective, or their thoughts, you're never going to come up with any innovative solutions."
>
> —Dr. Virginia Caine

Interviewer: *How did you get a good outcome on the project where you were trying to get the folks to come in for a syphilis test? How did that resolve?*

Virginia Caine: So that resolved by us saying, "Hey, you know what? Instead of me controlling the dollars to do this collaboration and addressing the syphilis problem, we needed to be more diverse. We had to have more diversity in our collaboration."

We really needed to get out and find those who were leaders in the community.

You know, your average person, Joe Blow person, livin' in the neighborhood–might be a janitor or whatever, but everybody in the neighborhood knows that person.

And there's a hierarchy a lot of times in the neighborhood. People who may not have a college degree, but they're well-respected. People come up to them, get their advice, blah, blah, blah, blah, blah.

So we decided to take the control of resources away from the health department, and give 80% back to the community—to the folks who we needed to impact, and let them come up with some of the strategies and interventions that would make a difference to them.

> "So there's a hierarchy a lot of times in the neighborhood. People who may not have a college degree, but they're respected.
>
> Involve them in your collaboration, let them come up with some of the strategies that would make a difference to them."
>
> —Dr. Virginia Caine

And this doesn't usually happen a lot.

You know, I think we got over a million dollars in federal funds. We actually gave over $800,000 of it to the community, and we let them decide what they thought was the best way to spend it.

Interviewer: How did they handle it?

Virginia Caine: They were phenomenal. We were considered one of CDC's best success stories that they've ever had, based on our process. And I don't think anyone else has done the process that way.

And you know what, it was fun because I learned a lot.

You know I got an MD degree, and yet you can have someone who may not have a high school degree with more expertise about what needs to be done in their neighborhood or their community in terms of some innovative strategies that can be very effective.

And yet I'm putting on them my experiences, how I grew up, which may be totally foreign to them from a cultural or language standpoint.

So it was a learning process for us. And you know, we have to be very careful about being judgmental in our communication, and then sometimes you have to look at your partners. There may be a static or elitist kind of participation in your collaboration.

So when you're lookin' at your partners around the table, to someone who's from a hospital system—their budget may be over a billion dollars—who thinks that they've got more power in the collaboration and things should always go their way, because they feel they're the more powerful partner. That approach may not move the dime at all in terms of what we want to impact. Because we may not have the right people at the table who understand the impact we need to make.

Interviewer: Have you ever had to walk away from a collaboration because it wasn't working?

Virginia Caine: Here's the thing, I have walked away from a collaboration that didn't work. I didn't walk away from the collaboration, I think the collaboration basically walked away from me.

We had a process called Building Healthcare Neighborhoods, and it started out fantastic, but I said, "You know folks, all around the table here is just hospital folks, and we really need to have representation from neighborhood associations."

"We're trying to attack these neighborhoods, but we don't have any folks with us from the neighborhoods. So we need to add people from the neighborhoods. I think education has been a major problem here in the neighborhoods so it would be nice to add someone from the educational arena too."

So I added those representatives, and we wanted someone from the provider healthcare standpoint to be part of this collaboration as opposed to just hospital administrators.

When I did that, my hospital partners got very, very angry with me, and they changed the date of when the meetings would be to the day of my board meeting, so there was no way I could continue to attend and be part of the collaboration process.

So essentially what happened was, they very effectively kept me out of the process.

I think they were very unhappy about the neighborhood folks making an input in terms of how the dollars were spent. Now I can honestly say that collaboration failed, and I know at the time it failed everyone around the table came back to me to tell me they'd made a mistake. They were sorry that it went downhill when the Health Department wasn't involved, because they weren't doing as good a job in terms of effectively communicating with the neighborhoods. The neighborhoods were very vocal and unhappy about the process, and they didn't feel that they were equal partners. They should have been part of shared decision making, but it wasn't perceived by them as shared decision making, so the process sort of folded.

Interviewer: *Perhaps the hospital interpreted what you were doing as rocking the boat. There were times you could smooth things over, and times you couldn't. Do you have any suggestions for persons reading the book on how to engage people in a way that they are comfortable changing their thinking?*

Virginia Caine: So here's the thing that I didn't realize, and I think this is really key. I know better now, but I didn't know it at the time.

You really need to have a better understanding of folks' perspectives and where they're coming from, and what their values and their expectations are. And you have to spend time with people to understand it.

You know we've got a shortage of time, but you need to take the time to build trust and get an understanding of where people are coming from.

I really didn't have a sense of how hospital administrators thought, at that particular time.

Now, we have all moved differently. We've all had our failures, and so we're now at a different stage. The hospitals have a better understanding of us, we have a better understanding of them, and our job is to try to close that loop; you know, how to have the hospital folks engage in their communities in an effective way, so they have an understanding of what's going on in them. I think the community benefits from this engagement are going to be tremendous.

When a hospital's looking at a patient, they look at their patients individually, or they only look at the patients that just come through their hospital doors, often sent from doctor's private practices.

As a health department, we look at communities as a whole, so we have a different perspective when we're looking at health services.

And so, we need to be able, each of us with our different language and different culture, we need to figure out a way to better understand each other, and work on both of our scripts in order to make a huge difference.

Interviewer: In order for someone to get you involved in a collaborative effort today, what does that collaborative effort need to have as its characteristics for you to say, "Yes, I'm going to take a look at doing this?"

Virginia Caine: For me, it's gotta be a critical health issue, or some complex health problem that needs to be solved. And I do think about more than just health services, because sometimes I have to work on an economic issue that may impact my health outcomes, or sometimes I have to work with the school districts about improving education that may help my health outcomes.

If I think it's an important issue, if I can see diversity as part of the collaboration, and if the people coming together for a common purpose can be effective, I'll be interested.

I look to see who is identified as being the partners, because you know, you've got some partners that you can work with till the cows come home, but you know that you're not going to get anywhere, because they may not be an effective partner, or a partner who respects perspectives from other people. So I do look to see who's involved in the collaborative process.

So if I think it's a good cause, and people seem to be committed and really want to get something done, you can probably get me involved in a collaborative process.

I'm always willing to try something new once.

Interviewer: Is there any other aspect of collaboration you'd like to comment on?

Virginia Caine: I talked about it, but let me just go at it a little bit stronger. You know, when we look at the demographics of our country, it's rapidly changing. And so, I think part of the problem we have for why some collaborations fail is because they don't value diversity.

And so, as a result of that, we're hampered in our efforts to come up with innovative solutions as opposed to the traditional interventions that are slow to move the dime.

> **"When we look at the demographics of our country, it's rapidly changing.**
>
> **Part of the problem as to why some collaborations fail is because they don't value diversity.**
>
> **And so, as a result of that, we're hampered in our efforts to come up with innovative solutions, as opposed to the traditional interventions that are slow to move the dime."**
>
> —Dr. Virginia Caine

And then I want to just say that a lot of times this is an unconscious process. It's not something that's deliberate. It's that sometimes we just don't think about bringing diversity to our collaborations.

Interviewer: Is there anything else you'd like to share on collaboration?

Virginia Caine: I think a collaboration will work if there's great continuous communication between collaborative partners, if everyone has a clear idea of what the goals of the collaboration are, and if there's shared decision making.

And then, if we meet together often enough to have many opportunities to interact with our partners that will help, because they need to know us if they're going to trust us, OK?

> **"We've got to have many opportunities to meet with our partners, because they need to know us if they're going to trust us."**
> —Dr. Virginia Caine

They need to know us to better understand us so trust can be established.

And then you have to have development of a well thought out strategy map. It's key, so that everyone knows who is doing what. Everybody's got to know what the other partner's doing, so they can see the progress being made on whatever initiative you're working on.

You know, you just can't be meeting a whole year, and nothing is happening.

You need to know what each one is doing, and what their level of expertise is to make that happen.

Virginia Caine: I've got just a few more things to say:

My story of success for collaboration—one was the Stamp Out Syphilis project that I told you about. We ranked #1 in the country for syphilis infections, and within 3 years we had over 100 some organizations involved to help us. Beauty shops, barber shops, even a laundromat and restaurants had messages on their menus, would you believe it, about syphilis.

And then we also were very effective with what we call our Indianapolis Healthy Babies Consortium, involving a lot of civic organizations, all the hospital systems, and organizations such as HUD (Housing and Urban Development).

You know, we got pregnant mothers referred by HUD to act as team leaders to help us with our strategies by telling us what we needed to do in order to get women into our facilities.

I hate to say it—it's terrible to say, but we ranked #1 with black infant mortality in the country, too.

That was a successful consortium and collaboration, because they told us pregnant women didn't feel like waiting for hours to be seen by a provider. They didn't have an appointment system. Everybody came at the same time and just sat and waited there with their kids, and you know, would wait for hours.

So we were able to change how some of the healthcare systems saw patients.

We also looked at our Women, Infant, and Children program that was offered by the health department. They told us we were set up more for the convenience of employees, as opposed to being convenient for the clients that we've served.

So you know, we had some hard truths told to us. If we wanted to make a difference, we had to change. So you find that a lot of self-evaluations and self-assessments sometimes might not present a glamorous picture of yourself or your organizations, and you might need to address those issues with some of these collaborations.

You need to have a thick skin, you have to have the ability to correct things, and you have to show people you are willing to make changes.

Interviewer: So what are 3 things that have to happen for collaboration to work?

Virginia Caine: Good communication and getting the right people involved.

You have to have the ability also to collect and analyze data, so that you know whether or not you're making a difference.

And you have to share strategies.

Now, I've been part of several collective impact projects, and we do a great job in several phases, I believe. We bring people together around a common purpose, we try to find a backbone partner if we can, and we select metrics and indicators to tell us whether or not we are making progress. You've got to have some kind of process to measure how effective your collaboration process is, and it's got to be visible enough for everybody to see.

But then, we can't make the leap to truly shared strategies in real time. Strategy needs to be shared in real time, maybe even electronically. You know sometimes you've got to be more sophisticated with social media, for some of us much more than we have been before. But it's also important to know how to communicate with those people who may not be social media conscious.

Anyone should be able to see who is doing what, and what is being accomplished. This also helps keep that momentum going—we gotta sustain it in order to achieve desired goals.

Interviewer: Why do collaborations fail when they fail?

Virginia Caine: Number 1, they lose their sense of purpose.

Number 2, communication is not effective among the partners.

Number 3, they don't trust their partners' skills, experiences, and what they bring to the table. I think there's a lack of trust or respect, and maybe a lack of value regarding their partners around the table.

I think that's why some collaborations fail.

The other thing that's unfortunate is that people can have different expectations for a collaboration, and because their expectations are not met in a timely fashion (sometimes people can have unrealistic expectations for a collaboration), the collaborations can fail.

I'll give you an example.

Some people will say, "Wow, your infant mortality is 15%."

Or your smoking rate is like 24%, and you say you want to knock that down to 15% in two years. Well that's just unrealistic. So you have people who don't have the expertise to know what's realistic based on the amount of resources available setting high expectations.

Now, hey, you give me 10 million dollars to work with every year, I'll start to get down to that going for a smoking rate of 10 to 15%. But if I've only got less than $200,000 to work on something, it will take me 4 to 6 years or longer to get to that point.

Sometimes we have unrealistic expectations.

Interviewer: *Your thoughts on why collaboration is needed today?*

Virginia Caine: You need to know that the demographics of our country's rapidly changing, and at the same time we've got limited funds. We have three times the healthcare costs compared to any comparable nation. We're considered the most sophisticated and most advanced country from a medical technology standpoint, but in terms of health outcomes, we do very, very poorly.

Because we have these limited dollars for healthcare, specifically public health, we really need that collaboration today, because we have to be more effective in getting the best outcomes for our community while controlling our healthcare costs.

And the only way to meet this challenge, you know, whether it's infant mortality, or whether it's the Flint, Michigan, environmental arena, we have to share resources.

We've got to be more efficient, we've got to be more effective, and we have to figure out how to pool our resources in order to get these larger, complex projects accomplished, because our cutbacks in public health have been tremendous over the past 8 years.

Look how CDC is fighting to get the funding to fight the Zika virus.

Now, I venture to say, it is easier to get a football team in Los Angeles, than it is to get money for public health. Something is wrong with that picture.

> **"We have to figure out how to pool our resources in order to get these larger, complex projects accomplished.**
>
> **It is easier to get a football team in Los Angeles, than it is to get money for public health. Something is wrong with that picture."**
>
> —Dr. Virginia Caine

CHUCK VEHLOW JR.

Charles M. Vehlow Jr. is director emeritus of Child Guidance & Family Solutions. As a consultant to the United Nations, he focused on crisis planning in war torn countries. His experience in collaboration spans 40 years of service focusing on development of a continuing system of services. He managed the merger of six agencies and countless collaborations.

Interviewer: Talk with me about collaboration.

Chuck Vehlow: Collaboration is the term used to describe a vision, an idea, a focused effort to combine two or more resources to form a new project.

When talking of collaboration, you have to define the extent of the collaboration or potential collaboration. At the simpler level, you have a project that can go through many phases to merger.

Interviewer: You talk about the pathway from collaboration to merger. Has it been your experience that long-term merger is often the last step?

Chuck Vehlow: Mergers may be a final step, or it could lead to other opportunities. The point I'm making is that there is a continuum between let's say a project level where two agencies discuss their visions and mutual interests so it may lead to a simple agreement or through a thoughtful process. A merger could be in their best interests.

Interviewer: You're saying the word merger has different meanings depending on where you are on that scale.

Chuck Vehlow: That's right. It takes mutual respect, focused discussions, and considerations of various views and rewards for the outcome. Leadership is a key element. A step-by-step process allows for all opinions to be expressed and considered. Jumping over the basic steps in the process doesn't allow for a fully designed collaboration or whatever product finally is considered.

Interviewer: What advice do you have for successful collaboration?

Chuck Vehlow: Successful collaboration is a dynamic process focusing on visions, goals, objectives, and the right people in the organization managing the process.

> **"Successful collaboration is a dynamic process focusing on visions, goals, objectives, and the right people in the organization managing the process."**
> —Chuck Vehlow Jr.

Interviewer: *You went through a process of merger with Child Guidance & Family Solutions, two agencies providing mental health services—one to children and adolescents, and the other to adults. What can you say about the process of collaboration and then merger?*

Chuck Vehlow: I think that collaboration is for more immediate goals, whereas mergers serve long-term goals. Of course there are no hard rules on this. When we got into the Family Solutions collaboration, we had no plans for a merger. The merger developed only after a whole series of opportunities emerged.

Interviewer: *What drove the collaboration of the two agencies? What were you both trying to achieve from a strategic perspective?*

Chuck Vehlow: Strategically, I think the vision was that we wanted to serve the family, and we wanted to serve the community. Child Guidance was primarily focused on children and did not have expertise in chemical dependency or some of the other services offered by Family Solutions. But Family Solutions had a "total family" orientation, which was attractive to Child Guidance. Child Guidance, whose name is now Child Guidance & Family Solutions, is an example of a merger that had developed over time.

Interviewer: *What did you need to overcome to accomplish the merger, in terms of board approval, staff getting on board, and even letting go of some leaders?*

Chuck Vehlow: Some of the success was that, from my perspective, it was not done on the executive level, except the oversight and planning. The experts in both agencies did the nitty-gritty work. When we got the right people together to talk about the right subject with similar goals, then the initial minor collaboration moved towards a merger. Board knowledge and consent was a key element. Weekly and monthly reporting to the board of trustees assured both agencies that all the work would not be in vain.

Interviewer: What are five things you'd say to someone considering collaboration for the first time?

Chuck Vehlow: Number one is a clear understanding of the specific reason the groups are meeting. Clarification of common language is important to make sure everyone is on the same page in the discussions. Understanding the value placed on an agency's values is critical and demonstrates mutual respect. The project of the Ropes Course, jointly sponsored by the YMCA and Child Guidance, fit well into the objectives of Child Guidance and YMCA, especially with the Y's faith-based mission.

Interviewer: So number one would be to understand that words can mean two different things in different organizations. What's a second?

Chuck Vehlow: Having executive discussions about possibilities is essential. A focused discussion of specific interests and general opportunities helps to focus key issues that are translated to boards and staff.

Number three is determining how it is going to benefit both organizations. Organizations don't have to benefit in the same way; one can benefit financially, and one can benefit from prestige. There has to be some payoff, and it has to fit within the organizations' business plans. As a sidelight, if an organization doesn't have a business plan, I'd be very leery of doing any collaboration with them.

The fourth is that as it progresses, the planning has to be discussed and considered very carefully. What are the major recorded steps, goals, and objectives of what we're planning?

> **"If an organization doesn't have a business plan, I'd be very leery of doing any collaboration with them."**
> —Chuck Vehlow Jr.

Interviewer: And the fifth suggestion?

Chuck Vehlow: The other critical thing is that in every organization you're dealing with, the human resources must be considered. Who is going to be the leader of the collaboration? Who is going to do the work?

Interviewer: We just covered five keys to success in collaboration. Have you ever been part of a collaborative effort that failed?

Chuck Vehlow: Yes.

Interviewer: What happened?

Chuck Vehlow: Looking back, I think that the key issue was that the directors did not have a clear vision of what they wanted to happen. That was communicated both verbally and nonverbally to staff.

Interviewer: Tell us a little bit about the nature of the collaboration you were trying to do.

Chuck Vehlow: We [Child Guidance] were trying to fit into a hospital's psychiatric services, and we did a lot of what I'd call due diligence, or risk work, and we found out where they were losing money. We also presented a plan that showed them where they could financially benefit. We could have developed a continuum between a community outpatient setting and an in-patient setting. Kids would be triaged in both agencies, saving resources of both organizations.

Interviewer: Why did it fall apart?

Chuck Vehlow: I think it's because it didn't involve both executives, and we didn't have a clear understanding of their business plans. Secondly, I believe both boards were not fully aware of the benefits and liabilities.

Interviewer: *What can you say about the way you need to manage your own ego and other people's ego when you are attempting collaborative efforts? What about the human factor?*

Chuck Vehlow: That's very important. It's not just the executives' ego; it's also the whole staff continuum right to the janitor.

Everyone has an ego, and you have to be very careful about showing people respect—showing them that they are participants in it and there is something for them, from the top to the bottom. One has to almost put their own ego aside from an executive point of view and ask how the other agency's ego is being addressed, as well as their own. And that should be talked out with executives as well as in work groups that actually do the grunt work of putting the collaboration together.

Interviewer: *Do you believe that public health organizations or other service organizations around the United States can accomplish more together than they could alone by utilizing collaboration in an astute manner? From your life experience, is the very concept that together you can do more than you can do alone valid or invalid?*

Chuck Vehlow: Well, it's a double-edged sword. One, I think it's a valid statement that collaboration does extend the services available, whatever the service or whatever the product. Collaboration is a more powerful system than an organization trying to do all things for all people. There are lots of examples of collaborations that save money, that save personnel, that save the visions.

But you do have to factor in the time it takes to collaborate, and this is often underestimated early on.

> **"You do have to factor in the time it takes to collaborate, and this is often underestimated early on."**
> —Chuck Vehlow Jr.

Interviewer: So it takes time and energy. It's kind of a formula. You have to do the math and determine whether you can live without the expertise that you need. If you find you do have to have the expertise, can you develop it in-house, or is collaboration the way you want to go? You actually have three options: don't do it at all, do it in-house, or collaborate.

Chuck Vehlow: I think that the collaboration is a much stronger vehicle to accomplish goals than a deal where you shake hands and hope for the best. In any collaboration, there should be a very specific risk assessment.

Interviewer: Is failure in collaboration damaging to your career? If you're a director of an organization like you were and you try to collaborate, and you get involved, and you get through the due diligence and implementation, and it fails, does it do damage to you, or not really? Can you afford to take a loss on collaboration as a leader?

Chuck Vehlow: I would say yes, you can afford to take a loss. It depends on whether you've done your homework with your board of trustees and other stakeholders. But just because a collaboration fails does not mean that it is a worthless effort. Yes, one can lose some personal goals, but one is better off for having tried and failed than to do nothing when a possible opportunity presents itself.

Interviewer: Are there any other ideas you want to share on collaboration?

Chuck Vehlow: I think that one of the issues with collaboration, extending all the way to merger, is how to communicate to staff because they are the stake holders in that organization as much as the director is. You can have a wonderful collaboration, but if you don't have the staff behind it, then you're going to fail. Obviously, they can't be at the executive level when it first starts; they may not even be at the second level where some overriding principles are discussed, and maybe not the third level where there's some discussion of committees and putting committees together, but after that point, one really needs to consider who are the stakeholders and how you communicate to them without causing disruption of your normal business but choosing the right people to do the work. At times, it is critical to use outside assistance to focus on one's process and to add expertise to the effort. I have found legal consultation is invaluable and keeps the effort from potential legal problems.

Interviewer: How do you do that?

Chuck Vehlow: The way I did it was to make sure my key executives were all informed well, and we would specifically say, "We need to tell the staff this." We always had that in the back of our minds because we knew staff would get upset because they'd think, "Maybe this is going to be a merger, and I'm going to be shut out, or fired, or whatever," and that of course is a possibility, but as the more intense planning goes on, the staff should know where the top executives' and board's thinking is heading.

> **"As the more intense planning goes on, the staff should know where the top executives' and board's thinking is heading."**
> —Chuck Vehlow Jr.

Interviewer: Talking about disaster planning, in 40 years you had a lot of collaborations—three big agencies. Some collaborations made it; some of them failed. Sometimes you have to get out of it as cleanly as you can. What are the keys to getting out in the best way possible when it's a failure?

Chuck Vehlow: One key is the board of directors. It always starts with that. They need to know the good, the bad, and the ugly. Secondly, make preparing for possible failure a part of the regular planning process. "If this doesn't work, who do we have to take into account?"

In social agencies it's United Way, and the ADM (Alcohol, Drug, & Mental Health) boards, and "the this and that"—all these collaborations. There's no way to keep them a secret; the rumors start, and you have to know something is out there, and you have to plan for a positive spin: "We tried this, and it didn't work. We're going to try something else."

DONNA PETERSEN, ScD, MHS, CPH

Donna Petersen has enjoyed over 30 years in the public health profession, earning her masters and doctoral degrees in the field from the Johns Hopkins University and serving in leadership positions in public health practice and in academia. She has served in various organizations devoted to public health excellence and quality, including the National Healthy Mothers, Healthy Babies Coalition; the Association for Maternal and Child Health Programs; the American Public Health Association; the Council on Education for Public Health; the National Board of Public Health Examiners; and the Association of Schools and Programs of Public Health. She owes her success to a profound appreciation of the art and the science of collaboration.

Interviewer: *In your opinion, what is the role of collaboration in life and in public health?*

Donna Petersen: We talk about this a lot because you know this; public health is not something anyone does alone. For some of our students, that's challenging because they like to work alone, and that's why they go into epidemiology or biostatistics, something they think that will allow them to be left alone. And we talk a lot about how the world doesn't work that way. It's everything from engaging the community and stakeholders and all those people throughout a planning process, but it's also within your organization—being a good colleague to the people you work with and reaching out to people you may not wish to reach out to. It's not thinking about the usual suspects but the unusual suspects in building coalitions and seeking ways to get things done.

> **"You know this; public health is not something anyone does alone."**
> —Dr. Donna Petersen

We can't get anything done in public health if we don't agree that there's work to be done. We have to agree there's a problem or a challenge or a need; you have to have that first.

Secondly, once you agree to that, then you have to agree on what the strategy is—what the solution is. And you can't do that alone; you can't sit in your office and decide what those things are.

You only do that by going out and listening, conversing with people, and negotiating, and trading—and all those things that I think those of us that have been in it a long time just do instinctively.

But that's kind of the bottom line; you can't be effective if you don't have people with you sharing the vision, sharing the energy, willing to contribute/advocate, whatever the words you like to use. It just doesn't happen.

Interviewer: *You talked about being a good colleague at work. Could you explain a little bit more about that within the context of your collaborations?*

Donna Petersen: Yes, because again, regardless of what you're doing externally, you're working with a core group of people. You've got the core team, and then depending on the situation, you may have to work with other folks in other divisions. We're all in bureaucracies, and when you go down the hall and knock on the door because you need something, you want them to look up and smile, "Hi."

> **"When you go down the hall and knock on the door because you need something, you want them to look up and smile, 'Hi.'"**
> —Dr. Donna Petersen

You don't want them to turn around and say, "I'm too busy for you." So part of that is just being a good person, being someone who's dependable, someone who will help somebody out because again, we're all in this together—whether you think you have a job that's very focused and very isolated. You don't.

There will come a day when suddenly what you're doing transects or crosses what other people are doing, or you're going to need some help from somebody else.

> "There will come a day when suddenly what you're doing transects or crosses what other people are doing, or you're going to need some help from somebody else."
>
> —Dr. Donna Petersen

I often tell my students stories about running into people in the most unlikely places. You're in the middle of a third world country, and you're in an airport, and somebody that you know comes towards you. Sometimes those are the happiest moments of your life. You're alone, and then you see somebody you know. You don't want that person to see you and turn.

I tell them that public health is an incredibly small field, and you had best be someone that people want to work with, that people care about and want to support, because we don't do anything alone.

You can't be effective outside if you're not effective inside, and often in public health, we're out there working on one thing, and we trip over something else, and we're not going to get our thing done until we address the other thing, and it might not be our thing—so we have to be able to go back to the office.

I've got a million stories about this.

You better know who to get to—and they better be willing to work with you and help you out because you're not going to get it done alone.

So externally, part of the negotiations when you're collaborating is, "Well, alright, I understand; you need this first, so I'll help you, and you'll help me." The same thing is true back in the office. It's the same set of principles to me.

Interviewer: *If you were giving a talk on "Five Rules For Getting Along With The People You Work With In Your Own Organization," what would those rules be?*

Donna Petersen: I think the bottom line is you do need to treat your colleagues well—with respect and with kindness—and part of that means you need to be available to them. You need to always listen first and talk next.

Interviewer: *But that's so hard to do, Donna. It's so hard to not talk!*

Donna Petersen: I actually learned this from my father: your best friend is dead air space—to sit there quietly—and people will eventually reveal what they're really upset about and what they really need.

You have to listen; you have to attend. You know we all know when you walk into the room and someone doesn't want to talk to you and they keep typing. Maybe there are people that you want to treat like that, but you have to think about that, even that, because someday you're going to need them, and they're going to turn away from you.

You also have to be patient. Things aren't going to happen at your speed or on your timeline, and you can't take things personally. Now I'm getting more into the leadership stuff, which isn't what you asked.

Interviewer: *No, I'm interested. Keep going!*

Donna Petersen: You cannot take things personally. Whatever the setting—you're in a meeting, you're on the phone, someone comes in your office, something is said, and someone reacts.

It's hard not to take things personally when someone's yelling at you, or someone's accusing you of something or questioning you. But I always tell people, "Don't take it personally," even if it is.

You don't gain anything by it. You have to let it go; you've got to try to figure out what the issue is, because you're not going to resolve it if it's emotions and it's personalities. You're only going to resolve an issue by resolving the issue, which means that's where you have to focus; that's where your energy has to be.

Be nice to people. How you make people feel at the end of the day is what they will remember.

> **"Don't take things personally, even if it is."**
>
> **Be nice to people. How you make people feel at the end of the day is what they will remember."**
> —Dr. Donna Petersen

Maya Angelou said, "At the end of the day, people won't remember what you did or what you said; they will remember how you made them feel." That's true.

Interviewer: Do you resent the fact that public health is underfunded?

Donna Petersen: Do I resent it? No, I don't resent it, because I think it's very difficult for people to understand what value we bring—what it is, what we do. People will often say, "We don't market ourselves well," or "We don't send the message well." I think we do a pretty good job.

It's very hard to grasp that we're trying to prevent things from happening and that you should pay for that.

Interviewer: Give me the short version of what public health professionals do.

Donna Petersen: I'm a fan of the old I.O.M.– the way they define public health, because I think it's simple and straightforward: "It's what we do as societies collectively to create conditions in which we can all be healthy." That's The Institute of Medicine's, The Future of Public Health, 1988.

I like it because it makes very clear that the responsibility for public health is a shared, societal, collective one. And again, you tell students: "I know you're getting a degree; you're going to be a public health professional, but you don't get to make the decisions. The public makes those decisions."

And I tell them, this is my made up thing: It's called public health because it's about the public–it's about everybody–but also because it belongs to the public. Only the public can decide what they're willing to do or have imposed upon them, or have restrictions placed on them. Only they decide. It's a very political process.

We don't get to say, "Well, obviously you want fluoride in your water, so we're going to put it in there, and you should just be happy, and stop complaining about it." That's not how it works, and you have to understand that, as a student going into this field, or anybody in this field, because otherwise you'll be so frustrated all the time and not be effective.

Interviewer: *Many of our interviews get into the details of the process of collaboration, which usually starts with determining a specific public health concern that needs to be addressed. You might not be able to handle this concern on your own, but you might have a shot of doing it with others, so you talk to the respective boards, develop lots of communication, and set benchmarks. Your own job performance might be judged in a little different light, and some amendments might be added to your job description. You might even need to have a back door strategy if the collaboration doesn't work. Within that admittedly minimal structure I just listed, what do you think is the hardest step to get through?*

Donna Petersen: Here is where my mind went when you asked that question. It's not necessarily the hardest; it's the one we don't spend enough time on, and that's actually coming to consensus on what the need is.

I'll give you an example I've used often in my career. When tattoo parlors started springing up all over the place, tattoos became popular, and I was working with a state I won't name. They were all over this. They wanted to get to the legislature and get some policies so that they could monitor these tattoo parlors.

It just came up in a training session I was doing in this particular state. I scrapped my whole agenda, and I swear to God it took me just under two hours to get the group to finally articulate that what they were concerned about was the transmission of blood-borne disease.

It's not the tattoo parlor; it's the blood-borne disease, right? Do you know the tattoo parlors? Has there been an increase in blood-borne disease? Do you know what I'm saying? Is there a real need, just because you don't happen to like tattoo parlors or you're worried with some appropriateness that there might be an issue there? I understand we're all about prevention.

What is it you're trying to do? And only when you figure that out, do you then say, "Okay now, what might be a solution to this?" And then to your point, you ask, "Who needs to be involved in this?"

Interviewer: I like your comment about need. It's interesting that the underlying issue was that there was a lack of knowledge on the part of the group about whether tattooing had any relation to blood-borne illness.

If somebody's not familiar with a topic, you're going to have a little trouble coming to consensus about whether or not this is something that should be done.

Donna Petersen: Yes, but I would also say that people get a mindset, and that's what they're on. They were so focused on these tattoo parlors.

The other example I often use is that I was working with a state school nurse group—and I don't care what problem you raised—more school nurses was the solution.

So it's sort of the opposite side of that same coin. I don't care what we said; more school nurses was always the answer. And so it gets back to people will jump to conclusions until you can clearly articulate the problem you're trying to address.

If someone has decided what the problem is, they've already decided what the solution is. They were on this because they wanted legislation so they could go into these tattoo parlors and do whatever they thought they needed to do. Until you can describe why you want to do that—why you want more school nurses—you can't move forward. Sometimes you have to get people out of their mindset.

> **"Sometimes you have to get people out of their mindset."**
> —Dr. Donna Petersen

It's not so much that they don't know, though that's often the case. If you've already decided that I need public health professionals, whoever they are—nurses, inspectors—to go into tattoo parlors, there's no room for collaboration. You've already decided what the problem is, and you've decided what the solution is.

So until you can open yourself up to really being able to articulate exactly what the need is and to back that up with evidence, then you've got a place to bring people together in a collaborative spirit to say, "What do we need to do about this?" Maybe there's some education that needs to happen. Maybe there's something about the people who manufacture the products that tattoo artists use.

Interviewer: How do you know if an issue you're considering that has been vetted as both legitimate and worthy has a chance to be addressed successfully through collaboration? Conversely, what are the warning signs that a given issue could not be addressed through collaboration?

Donna Petersen: Obviously, if the problem is urgent, there is no time for that. If there's a disease outbreak and you need to get the population inoculated immediately, there's no time to be nice and get people involved [for a collaborative process]. So there are those events, disasters, where you should have collaborated beforehand so everyone knows what they're doing, like large-scale food-borne and other disease outbreaks. The public health department has the authority to act on them, and they probably should.

I would argue there should have been conversation well ahead of time in anticipation of those kinds of urgent situations so that you mobilize your partners and all that.

I'm hard-pressed to think of a scenario that is not an immediate, urgent, disaster situation that doesn't gain something from reaching out to somebody [to collaborate].

Of course, leaders in public health will focus on organizations and board-to-board communications when considering collaborative efforts. I tend to be more roll-up-your-sleeves-in-the-dirt type of person, so I don't always think about how I get this lofty institution to collaborate with this other lofty institution. I'm more just on the ground. Who do you need to work with to get something done?

Every time you do that, you build a relationship that should then make it easier when you're at the level where you do want your board signing some sort of agreement, there's already an established relationship there. There's a level of familiarity and trust.

Interviewer: *When you want to share a vision on something that you think needs to be addressed in public health, and you're going to use collaboration, do you meet with the people and go for coffee, or a meal? Do you call them on the phone? What works best?*

Donna Petersen: All those things. If you know the person, you're going to call them up and invite them out for coffee or a drink or something. If you don't, you'll call them, and you may invite them to meet somewhere, maybe somewhere more formal. If you've already got a group going, you might say, "Wow, you know who we forgot? We didn't invite anybody from the police." Then we might call and say, "We'd love to engage you; join us in our meeting." It's an iterative thing, and the level of formality or informality is more related to the relationship you already have with that person.

When I worked for a state health department, I spent a lot of my time cultivating those relationships whenever there was a reason to do so because I knew someday I would need it.

One of the biggest frustrations was, I'm in the health department, and we're pretty stable. There's not a lot of turnover, but over in the welfare side of the house, they were coming and going left and right.

If you weren't best buddies with the head of the Medicaid program or the mental health program and substance abuse, it was very difficult for me to get anything done. So I had parties and invited them to my house as a new friend because you have to get to know people.

I remember this one woman. It was all I could do to get her to thaw. She was so tense and stiff and formal, and I needed to be able to relate to her. I tried all my normal tricks, but they didn't work, and then we had this conversation, and she mentioned she had a DPA, which I had never heard of, a Doctor of Public Administration degree.

And we got talking, and I said, "You know, it's funny, I have a Doctor of Science, and I have friends who are physicians, and I have friends with PhDs, and I have friends with DVMs," and then I said, "It would be fun for us all to get together. How does Wednesday work?" and she said, "Yeah! That would be fun."

I'm like, okay! I got a group of women together [laughs] who had all their different degrees, and it was the first time I saw her let go, even for a minute. But that was important because I had to be able to work with her.

That's a different kind of example than what you're getting at, but I think if you're serious about what you're doing, and you recognize the power of partnership, you've got to be cultivating relationships.

If I had waited to call her when I needed her for some collaborative program, it would have never gone anywhere. I think that we always have to be thinking of it.

I say to my students, "If you are staying in the office all day long, there's something very wrong with you or your boss, or something." It's not how the world works.

Interviewer: There was a time when you thought about your future in public health—at the beginning when you were getting involved in a leadership position—and you had this idea in your mind about collaboration. What ended up being different between what you thought collaboration would be about and what you now see it's about based on years of experience?

Donna Petersen: What's different is when it's young, and it's new, and we're very naive, and we think others are thinking the same way we are. It gets back to need. As an example, we might say, "It's so obvious to me that we all need to rally around breastfeeding," and other people don't get excited about that, or don't see that they have a role.

You read it in a book; you go out, you find the stakeholders, you get them together, you form a coalition, you get all the little tips about keeping minutes, and you send out a newsletter.

But then when you're actually out there trying to do this, you have to learn that it's not that they don't necessarily appreciate what you're concerned about or see it's important; there are other competing priorities out in the world.

So others may be more concerned at the moment about fraud and abuse or about getting people enrolled in health care coverage. They understand breastfeeding; they understand they might have a role in it, but it's not where they are right now.

You can't hold a sort of Pollyanna-ish view of the world—that is it's so obvious and everyone understands these things—it's not. Again, if I think I need the WIC Program [Women, Infants, and Children] to be on board with the breastfeeding effort, which I do, then I'm going to have to figure out if can I help them do something now that would help them be in a better position to be more engaged.

And then in a much more you know, just kind of "quid pro quo" kind of way, if I do help them do something, then they'll feel obligated to do something for me. Sometimes you know you kind of have to play those games. Again, it gets back to the personalities, and sometimes people are great to work with and happy to help you out; other times you have to either coax or trick them into it to, almost to say, "Heyyyy! Just callin', you know, remember all that good work we did on X? Well, I really need your help on Y." Most people are good people and will respond.

Interviewer: *Is there anything else you'd like to talk about?*

Donna Petersen: One thing that you said that struck me that I haven't thought about was the back door—when you pull out. I don't know if it's come up before, but there are occasionally ethical dilemmas that arise when you're working in a collaborative effort where people might not share the values that you share, or might not have as much difficulty with something that you feel is unethical. That happens often, in my experience. I've never really thought about a back door, but I have exited myself when I feel like my involvement either puts my organization in a precarious position, in an unfavorable light, or is so in conflict with my values as a person and professional that I can't continue.

Those things happen, and you don't get mad and storm out. You thank them and say, "Because of where this is going, I don't think I can contribute in any meaningful way."

CASWELL A. EVANS JR., DDS, MPH

Caswell A. Evans Jr. is currently the associate dean for Prevention and Public Health Sciences at the University of Illinois, Chicago College of Dentistry. He is also a faculty member in the UIC School of Public Health. Previously, he served as executive director and project director for *Oral Health in America: A Report of the U.S. Surgeon General*. He is a past president of the American Public Health Association, the American Association of Public Health Dentistry, and the American Board of Dental Public Health.

Interviewer: *Can you share some of your observations about collaboration with me?*

Caswell Evans: All leaders must work with and through other people because when you get down to it, there is very little that we can actually accomplish working single-handedly as individuals.

We might have a concept as an individual, but to actualize it—to make it happen—requires collaboration and working with and through others.

It works best when the idea or the purpose is more or less given away so that everybody sees themselves in the purpose, the initiative, and in the outcome—and embraces it from that perspective.

And leaders who portray that they can do one thing or another single-handedly, and it only takes their particular leadership and their particular individual skills to achieve something are not being truthful to the reality. Or they don't see the reality that it really takes collaboration, cooperation, and multiple people to achieve even the simplest objectives.

I see that from a leadership perspective, and that's particularly pertinent in public health, which is by definition, a collective reality—a group reality, a collaborative reality—whether you're at the federal, state, or local level.

Interviewer: Suppose you ran into someone who had not bought into the idea of collaboration. What would you say to them to coach them to understand the importance of working with other people?

Caswell Evans: In a very practical sense, it is simpler and less taxing on one's mind and body—and stress—to work collaboratively with others, number one.

Number two, while we tend to all think that we have a situation fully-scoped and fully-measured, invariably when you work with others, you get a perspective that is new and sometimes quite influential to the outcome you want to achieve. So working with others gives you a much broader sense of the reality of the situation you're facing and frequently brings in alternative strategies or companion strategies that an individual, despite their level of knowledge of a situation, may well miss.

> "Working with others gives you a much broader sense of the reality of the situation you're facing."
> —Dr. Caswell A. Evans Jr.

So sharing the load, sharing the burden, and being capable of sharing the glory of the outcome is also part of the joy of partnerships. It's one thing to celebrate an accomplishment alone; it's another thing to celebrate an accomplishment with a group of people who have also been invested in that outcome.

Interviewer: Sometimes there's an assumption that when we discuss collaboration, everybody understands why the concept is valuable. Some of our interviews have made clear, however, when you sometimes get into a situation where you're working with someone—let's say fresh out of a masters program or in some other situation where they haven't had a lot of collaborative experiences the question becomes, "How do you coach someone who has never engaged in collaboration to engage their spirit in the effort?"

Caswell Evans Jr.: I tend to view that kind of a question through mentoring, depending upon the nature of the relation between the individuals. If there's someone who is entering into the field or entering a set of issues to which they are committed but they really have not had the opportunity for experience, an experienced collaborator can say, "Involve me in this process. You take the lead; I'll follow, and you can begin to appreciate how collaborative relationships are developed, how they are nurtured, and you'll see the value of collaboration," because collaboration takes a lot of care and feeding.

> "Collaboration takes a lot of care and feeding."
> —Dr. Caswell A. Evans Jr.

There's some give and take because whenever you solicit an individual, a group, or an organization to collaborate with you on an initiative, you need to expect that down the line, there's going to be a quid pro quo, and they will call on you to collaborate with them on their own initiative.

> **"Whenever you solicit an individual, a group, or an organization to collaborate with you on an initiative, you need to expect that down the line, there's going to be a quid pro quo, and they will call on you to collaborate with them on their own initiative."**
> —Dr. Caswell A. Evans Jr.

Collaboration needs to be seen as a two-way endeavor, and mentoring is the best way to introduce someone to that type of relationship if they've not been in one before.

Just say, "This is something you seem to be interested in learning, and here's an opportunity to learn. Just join in and observe, and over time you will have an opportunity to become a full participant. Very quickly, you'll find that you will be in a position to establish collaborative relationships on an issue of your choosing.

Interviewer: So the best way to understand the benefits of collaboration is to provide the experience of being in a collaborative effort.

Caswell Evans: Yes, exactly.

Interviewer: What do you think makes you a good collaborator?

Caswell Evans: I am particularly good at two things: one is crafting a persuasive vision that attracts people to an initiative that requires some collaboration.

I'm very good at drawing the vision that shows everyone who might be involved what their piece of that vision could be.

Part of that is also what I call "giving it away." From a leadership perspective, once the vision is crafted, you've got to be prepared to let it go to the point that everyone has to see the vision as a collective, but they've got to interpret the vision from their own perspective, and say, "Within this vision, I see this particular piece as being ours, *or* mine, and this is what I can do with this piece."

> **"You've got to let go. Once the vision is crafted, everyone has to see the vision from their own perspective and say, 'This is what I can do with this piece.'**
>
> **Then let them bask in the glory of their accomplishment."**
>
> **—Dr. Caswell A. Evans Jr.**

Part of letting go is once the vision is out there, you've got to let go. I'm good at letting go and letting everyone see themselves in the vision—see themselves in the movie, what role they want to play and be able to let them bask in the glory of accomplishing that vision, as opposed to always being "mine," and about me and what I want to do. It's got to be about all of us.

Part of it is selling my idea to others so that they also see it as their idea.

I like it most when somebody else takes credit for an idea that I knew that I generated, but they embraced it and made it theirs. They were at one with it, and that's great too.

> **"I like it most when somebody else takes credit for an idea that I knew that I generated . . . but they embraced it and made it theirs."**
> —Dr. Caswell A. Evans Jr.

When I was director of public health for Los Angeles County, my greatest pleasure was when somebody took an initiative that we were working on that I had developed in collaboration and took it over as theirs. I said, "Now, it's got legs; they've given it legs, and they're going to run with it. That's great! We go on to the next item."

Interviewer: Let's put that in terms of "How To." How do you help someone see where they fit?

Caswell Evans: I know to some degree those whom I collaborate with. I know what they do, and I know their set of objectives. While I can't exactly walk in their shoes, I can somewhat put myself in their place. So I try to outline for them what I see as the value that they would derive from the collaborative vision and try to explain it as best I can, and they will amplify that.

Rarely will they say, "No, I don't see that at all. I see something different."

They will tend to say, "Well, I see that—and I see some additional things."

So I think it's a matter of kind of crafting the vision, and within that vision, crafting specific avenues that describe what value each of the collaborators will get out of the partnership in terms of their own particular interests and use.

Interviewer: *Do you have any tips on how to help people to internalize their vision of their place in the collaboration?*

Caswell Evans: I don't know that I do that; I think they do that. We all come with our own sets of visions and objectives. I may know some, but I don't know them all. I think it's a matter of describing that vision as rich and pertinent to their interests as you possibly can. Recognizing that they will be interpreting your words, they will see the vision for themselves, and if you kind of give them a string they will hold onto, somehow or another, they'll weave that string into a rope.

Interviewer: *I see you as a professional who provides a lot of mental space for the other person to think or speak into. Do you see yourself that way?*

Caswell Evans: I do, and that's really what I'm trying to say. That is part of pulling back and giving it away. You've got to give space to all of your collaborating partners so they can craft their own vision within the larger vision. They not only need to see the value of achieving the overall objective but also that they come out with a set of values and gems that are particularly relevant for them. When you pull back, your partners will add to the initial vision, and in some regards, that vision can change, and you've got to be comfortable with that change. It's important to recognize that change should not be totally detrimental to the original purpose; it will change, and morph, and grow. In that sense the vision will become even richer, and you ensure the greater buy-in of a partner.

Now you multiply that by four, five, or six partners in an endeavor, and the endeavor definitely begins to change shape. You must be comfortable with evolution. If that does not occur, you do not really achieve an effective partnership.

Interviewer: *To allow someone to speak about their vision and really hear opinions that are different from yours, you have to be an excellent listener. Where in your life did the seed of being a good listener get started?*

Caswell Evans: I had good role models, but I believe the more important lesson came to me throughout my career as a leader in public health, particularly when an issue was occurring on my watch, but the issue itself was well out of my area of expertise. So the best I could do was to listen carefully to the experts, gather opinions as best I could, and eventually make a decision, not about the scientific facts, but about the strategy to follow to resolve the issue.

Interviewer: *You come across as a respectful gentleman. Were you always respectful of others?*

Caswell Evans: Yes, I believe so, even though I've never really thought about that. I grew up in Harlem in a pretty rough and tumble environment where you had to learn to size people up in situations very, very quickly because safety and longevity depended upon that skill. I guess I was respectful in those days of the process and the environment, and that probably helped me develop a sense of respect and appreciation.

But certainly in my career in public health, you really have to be respectful of the public and media environments you're in.

You've got to respect those things that you know factually and from your own personal training, and respect those things that you don't know anything really about but happen under your umbrella. You've got to respect what you know and respect what you don't know.

> **"You've got to respect what you know and respect what you don't know."**
> —Dr. Caswell A. Evans Jr.

But in my role, I was responsible for what goes on, whether I was factually up to date on the situation or not.

Interviewer: *Stylistically, you remind me of what is called a "cool cucumber with a long fuse." Now that's a compliment! I get the impression that it would be really difficult for someone to tick you off. I think part of your success in collaboration is that you're a cool cucumber.*

Caswell Evans: I don't know about the cucumber, but I tend to be cooler than hotter, and I have found quite honestly that I have made my most serious mistakes when I have acted in the heat of the moment. So I have learned to count to ten, or go get a drink of water, or take a walk around the block, or whatever it is. I have tried not to react in the heat of the moment. I'm not always perfect at that; every now and then I make a mistake.

Because public health issues can become so contentious, you realize that when people make vehement points during a heated discussion, they're coming at an issue from the way they see things. It's important to understand what they see and how they see it and put it in perspective.

I go back to some of the earliest days of HIV and the Act Up Movement and things of that sort, and those of us working at the health department in Los Angeles were recipients of some of their attention. You have to learn in some of those environments to put aside the actions and try to understand the thought that goes on behind the actions and how they're viewing the world. That helps slow you down as well.

Interviewer: *Suppose you're in a meeting with six people, and somebody says something that you totally disagree with. What do you do?*

Caswell Evans: I have no hesitancy to speak my mind, and if someone is way off base in terms of my estimation, I'll give my viewpoint. I do that also with the people that report to me. I've always told anyone that I've recruited or interviewed for a position that works for me that I don't want people to rubber stamp what I say.

I want people who can see issues from their own perspective, and if they think I'm off base, they need to let me know what their opinion is. I've never thought that I've got 100% clarity on all issues.

> **"I've never thought I've got 100% clarity on all issues."**
> —Dr. Caswell A. Evans Jr.

Interviewer: We were talking about what you thought you were good at in the world of collaborative effort. Let me ask about the other side. What do you find most challenging?

Caswell Evans: I find day-to-day, routine administration most challenging. I'm always about searching out new horizons and taking on new challenges. I'm not very good at the day-to-day stuff, and I don't pay a lot of attention to it. Sometimes it comes back to bite me, but I find that most of it is not particularly consequential.

I have to practice being patient because I'm always eager to move things along as quickly as possible. I have to recognize that sometimes things just take the time that they take.

I'm not as patient as I'd like to be. Those are two things that come to mind.

Interviewer: So you're vision-oriented, but the details drive you nuts, and you have to constantly tell yourself to be patient. Have you found that you have to really focus on due diligence, keeping in touch with people, and communicating with them in collaborative efforts?

Caswell Evans: No, that portion is part of the whole process. What I meant by day-to-day administration is time keeping and record keeping—just the mundane things. I've never paid much attention to that.

But here's an example of the importance of the care and feeding of collaborations by staying in touch with folks. We have a collaboration with Muhimbili University in Dar es Salaam, Tanzania, where we're sending five students who will be going there for a four-week period to provide clinical care. It's a kind of culture immersion. There are all kinds of details in dealing with Muhimbili University and their dean that have to be resolved.

So I immerse myself into that type of detail—like setting up the location and having it be fulfilling because it is part and parcel to our collaboration. It's just the mundane, routine, day-to-day kind of administrative . . .

Interviewer: *Non-humanistic things. When it comes to people, you work well with them; if it's a time-keeping thing, it's not your cup of tea.*

Caswell Evans: I must say it's worked for me. I don't recall every being badly burned over that.

Interviewer: *Do you think someone going into a collaborative effort would do well to think about what they're good at and not good at?*

Caswell Evans: It's always helpful to have a sense of yourself and to know your strengths and weaknesses. You may want to turn some of your weaknesses into strengths, and for other weaknesses, you may just say, "I'm pleased to leave that be a weakness."

I know my insensitivity to routine administrative matters is a weakness. I'm not about to address it; let it be a weakness.

AMY LEE, MD, MPH, MBA

Dr. Amy Lee is professor of family and community medicine at Northeast Ohio Medical University. She is also the program director for the Consortium of Eastern Ohio Master of Public Health program, a consortial degree program that has had up to six university partners.

Interviewer: What are some of your ideas and views on collaboration?

Amy Lee: You have to really want to collaborate, but you also have to be pretty passionate about your goal because it's a lot of effort to be able to collaborate. It's very time consuming. It takes a lot of your energy, so if you don't enjoy working with the collaboration, you're going to be awfully fatigued at the end of the day.

I tend to draw energy from people, which is the definition of an extrovert. So I usually feel pretty energized at the end of the day because I love what I do. I enjoy the collaborative aspects of my work, but it does take tons of time. I'm always following up with people to try to get information from them or trying to enable what they do into the collaborative. It takes a lot of patience. You can't be too serious about yourself; otherwise, you're going to be pretty deflated at the end of the day. You just can't take things personally. I think some people may call that humility.

Interviewer: What determines if an individual or group is a good choice to collaborate with?

Amy Lee: It's like looking for a job; you have to do your homework and figure out what and for whom you're going to be working. You want to understand their characteristics—where they're coming from—and that way, you can hopefully serve both of your interests.

Sometimes you don't really have a choice about who you need to work with for a collaborative; it may be just based on positions. For example, in my case, I'm working with educational institutions, and there are particular people in particular positions that you want on a committee because they are equivalent to other roles at each partner university. So whoever comes into that position is the person that you work with, whether that person is pleasant or unpleasant.

Interviewer: And the nature of your collaborative effort is essentially different institutions of education working together on public health master degree programs. And some go in, and some go out. When they set up their own school, they go out.

Do you find that it's difficult to keep people interested in the kinds of collaborations you're involved with?

Amy Lee: Actually, it hasn't been too difficult because it's a pretty defined goal. It's a degree program, and everybody's in that business—they're all into academic programs. So far, it's been relatively successful, and when I mean successful, I mean it hasn't lost money; we continue to have students. The mission of improving the health of the community is a good one. We haven't caused problems. As long as we don't have too many problems that we bring to the table and people feel good about the mission, we've been able to maintain the program. The consortium is ongoing, despite local competition and a lot of turnover in program committees and even the leadership positions.

As long as you have that original buy-in from the original leaders—the presidents of the institutions—and they say, "Make it go," then it goes. That initial buy-in from the leaders was very important, at least in our collaboration.

> "As long as you have that original buy-in from the original leaders—meaning the presidents of the institutions—and they say, 'Make it go,' then it goes."
> —Dr. Amy Lee

Interviewer: When would you conclude that a collaboration needs to be terminated? You might accomplish your goal. Are there other factors people should look at—a shift in the needs of the members or change of leadership at the top?

Amy Lee: If you severely lack a resource to make it go, perhaps another reason might be that people just lose interest in the particular goal if you aren't meeting the goal the way you originally intended.

For example, my collaborative is to provide accredited public health education to students in a collaborative way. If for some reason, people just decided not to apply to the program—if we didn't have any students—that wouldn't be achieving the goal.

Another reason might be if the quality of the teaching went down a lot, and we weren't able to graduate students who were able to get good jobs, that would be a problem. So if for some reason, we aren't meeting our goal, then we have to take a hard look at what we need to change to enable us to meet the goal. Another reason might be if we just don't have resources to be able to do it or the people with the passion to be able to do this.

A change of leadership does not necessarily mean that the collaboration needs to be terminated. As long as enough people have a buy-in to the goal and mission, then it can continue. All of our program university partners have different presidents and graduate deans from when the program first started. If I ever decide to leave, I would make sure there is succession planning and documentation on how to run the program. I would also want to make sure that my replacement was passionate about directing the program.

Interviewer: One of the topics we're thinking of adding to the book is a little more general than collaboration—getting along with people. Do you have any input on that?

Amy Lee: When I started in this effort, I was a physician who had recently quit my practice, and I was hired into this position to put together this collaborative master of public health program. I really didn't know very much about influencing people and getting along with other people. What I did was get a good mentor and talked to people who have experience in being able to negotiate, understand the politics, and just help me understand how to get along to be able to pull it together.

I've also read a lot of books, but I still have a lot to learn.

Interviewer: *What were the most powerful concepts you learned?*

Amy Lee: Understand where the other people are coming from. One book that I read was *Getting More* by Stuart Diamond. One concept was about seeing the pictures in other people's heads—in other words, what their perspective is and where are they coming from, so that you can try to approach the situation from their perspective in addition to getting what you want.

Keeping good communication lines is also important. When you're in a collaborative, you can't keep everything to yourself; you have to make sure that others are aware. They may not respond to you if you provide information, but at least you made the effort to keep them in the loop and keep them on top of what's going on with the collaborative.

Flexibility and adaptability help as well. There are so many different people that you deal with on a day-to-day basis, and everybody has a different approach. Everybody has a different way of communicating, so being rigid from your own standpoint just won't work.

You have to make sure you are fairly adaptable to other people's styles, and you can't shut other people off. You have to make them feel valued because of their input on what's going on.

You're not going to please everybody because you have to sometimes go one direction. You can't go all the directions that everybody wants you to go into, but at least you want to try to make people feel good about participating in the process.

So being able to make people feel good about being a part of the collaborative is very important as well.

Interviewer: *How do you manage anger, or let's say discomfort?*

Amy Lee: Actually, I was just about to say before you asked that question, that another characteristic of being a part of a collaboration is not to get too emotional about what's going on.

You can't take things too personally; you can't lay your emotions on the table. I can tell you I don't usually get angry unless for some reason, I'm highly stressed. I may get upset, but I don't get red-faced angry.

Maybe it's because of my perspective. I was a practicing OB/GYN physician before I got training in public health and came to NEOMED to direct the MPH program.

And the times of stress as an OB/GYN were when somebody died. I can tell you in academia, nobody dies—at least as a result of anything that you do in academia.

As long as people aren't getting seriously maimed, injured, or killed, nothing really is worth that much stress. Sure, there are a lot of deadlines and people that you want to please, but when you've been through the kind of stress of, "Oh my gosh, somebody could die," situations in academia just don't compare. So I just put it in perspective.

Interviewer: *What else can you say about getting along with other people? Some of our readers are skilled in getting along with people, and some aren't. Those who aren't will need help.*

Amy Lee: I didn't realize that I needed to get along with people until I got into this collaborative effort, and part of it is just being aware that you need to get along with other people and be interested in how other people get along with others.

My favorite book to this day is Dale Carnegie's *How To Win Friends and Influence People*. Even though it was published in 1936, the stories still ring true. I've read a lot of books after that, and they've given more scientific explanations and added more stories, but it still gets down to that basic concept: people are people, and they want to feel valued.

And in order to be able to influence people, you need to get along with them.

> "My favorite book to this day is Dale Carnegie's *How To Win Friends and Influence People*. Even though it was published in 1936, the stories still ring true.
>
> I've read a lot of books after that, and they've given more scientific explanations and added more stories, but it still gets down to that basic concept: people are people, and they want to feel valued.
>
> And in order to be able to influence people, you need to get along with them."
>
> —Dr. Amy Lee

I found out my Myers-Briggs type indicator is an ESTJ, and I didn't know I was an extrovert until later in life. When I was young, I was terribly shy because of my cultural background. I now understand that other people have different ways they approach situations than I do and have different Myers-Briggs profiles. These differences can sometimes cause conflict when working together. So even though I am aware people have different styles and approaches, I am still learning the best ways to reach a common goal together.

However, I enjoy interacting with people. Observing and reading how others get along and how they influence people has just been a subject of interest to me and continues to be. You have to be a life-long learner on this subject.

I've even given some workshops to people at health departments on influencing others. Some of it's very basic. I mean, we're all human, and we all respond to people understanding where we're coming from; it makes us feel valued.

> **"We're all human and we all respond to people understanding where we're coming from; it makes us feel valued."**
> —Dr. Amy Lee

Interviewer: These are simple ideas but not easy to do.

Amy Lee: Yes, it is hard to do. However, it can be as easy as calling others by their name. I don't have the best memory for names, but sometimes if I pay attention enough, I can retain that name.

People like Bill Clinton are incredible at being able to remember people's names years after they have met them. That really requires attentiveness to people, and I'm still trying to develop that. I'm still trying to develop my listening skills. I think I tend to be almost ADD. I'm listening, and hearing, and seeing a lot of things at one time because I'm trying to multi-task—which, by the way, people cannot do. You literally cannot multi-task.

So I'm trying to be able to focus on what I'm doing at that point in time. For example, I'm talking to you, and I need to try to focus on that, rather than thinking of many things at one time.

I'm trying to develop the ability to be attentive to the person I'm with.

And I think being heard makes people feel good.

Interviewer: *To switch gears for a minute, let me ask you why Bill Keck has been so successful at collaboration in his lifetime? You've had the opportunity to work closely with him.*

Amy Lee: Bill Keck has been a mentor of mine from day one in my career in public health. And he has taught me so much and opened so many opportunities for me. He listens, and he's been able to hone techniques through the years that perhaps some people wouldn't be willing to try.

But he always has a reason, evidence, and good rationale behind the decisions that he makes, and it's difficult to argue with him.

He's also very kind.

I think he believes in looking at the positive sides of people first before looking at the negative sides of people.

Interviewer: *Why do you think he's ideally suited for collaboration? Because he does a lot of it, and he's good at it!*

Amy Lee: People can trust him; he inspires trust. He listens to you. He's also very professional. Professionals are responsive; they get back to you, and they listen to what you say.

They may not follow through with every idea they hear because they get input from a lot of people. However, I feel like he's heard me. He has that quiet sense of, "I've listened to you, and I'm observing it, and I will certainly incorporate it into what I'm thinking."

Interviewer: *You feel that truly he did listen.*

Amy Lee: It's what I was talking about before—about making people feel valued. He makes me feel valued because he listens to me.

But I think a big factor of why he's been successful through his career is that you can trust him because he'll always go back to excellent rationale/reason. He doesn't fly off the handle.

I've never seen him get angry. I have never seen him display full-blown emotions on the table—wearing it on his sleeve. He's very even-keeled.

He has a really good sense of thinking through particular problems and situations. I have been the luckiest person to be able to call Bill my mentor and friend.

MARY JANE STANCHINA

Mary Jane Stanchina is executive director of the Six District Educational Compact in Ohio, which provides collaboration and sharing of resources among six school districts. This compact has been in existence for 46 years.

Interviewer: *If you were giving a presentation to 500 students or those interested in collaboration, what would you tell them?*

Mary Jane Stanchina: Collaboration is about people, and it's about those faces coming together to discuss, identify, and problem solve issues. Those issues could be good, negative, or even almost in-between issues.

Collaboration is a communication strategy and a process that can be extraordinarily effective if people understand the parameters and guidelines about it.

Interviewer: What are good questions to ask when talking with someone you are considering engaging in a collaborative effort?

Mary Jane Stanchina: Identifying the need is the first step. Generally when we do collaborative projects, it's built around a type of need. That need could involve all six of our districts, or maybe not.

Interviewer: How much time does it take to lock down need?

Mary Jane Stanchina: That depends on the topic. If it's a crisis, it would be immediate; if not, and it's something we'll feel is "a good thing for students, for staff, or the community," then it might be a longer process of developing the identified need.

Interviewer: Let's pretend there's a continuum from not very much of a need to a very compelling need. What advice can you give to help people figure out whether the need is enough to warrant the effort it takes for collaborative effort? How do you personally figure that out? Is it a gut thing, or an intuition, or is there some kind of matrix based on criteria?

Mary Jane Stanchina: There could be numerous answers for all these questions! Many times it is an intuitive construct. However, there may be other people in the six districts thinking about the same topics and concerns when they come together for professional dialogue to identify these topics. This dialogue, a valuable asset of the Compact structure, is often the basis for a need to be presented for further research.

Interviewer: Do you think people's perception of need is accurate? Since it all begins with need, we must determine if it's a real need or not. Do you find that most of the time, when a need starts coming to the surface in discussions that it is legitimate?

Mary Jane Stanchina: Most of the time, it's been a timely or legitimate issue.

Interviewer: *Did you ever have one that wasn't?*

Mary Jane Stanchina: There have been questions brought to us like, "Why don't we do this? or "Why don't we do that?" and in looking at those questions, there wasn't enough documentation or interest in our six districts to move forward.

Interviewer: *So you don't use a checklist or a numerical tool that shows if you get a score of 80 or more, you proceed?*

Mary Jane Stanchina: No, we do not, but you do use research and data analysis for some projects.

Interviewer: *That sounds just a little bit loosey-goosey, doesn't it?*

Mary Jane Stanchina: Yes, it may. Understanding the concept of what I refer to as "where the rubber meets the road" can be important to the decision making process. As an example, early in my time in the Compact, several students died from suicides and car accidents. This was before school districts were required to have crisis plans in place. Compact district personnel went to the "districts in crisis" and provided support services to students and staff. They helped with whatever was necessary at that moment, hour, or day. It was the right thing to do at the time.

Interviewer: *That one certainly is a crisis.*

Mary Jane Stanchina: Another example of Compact collaboration occurred related to submitting a grant to the Ohio Department of Education. We had discussed the topic for many years—and now, here was the opportunity. We had twelve days to prepare the grant. After meeting with various administrators it came down to, "Are we moving forward with this, or are we not?" The answer was, "Let's go." In this scenario they committed to providing us the data and to trusting those writing the grant with their ideas. People from the districts and an area university gave of their time for the venture. The outcome? We were awarded the grant.

Interviewer: Are *"emotional buy-in and emotional commitment" critical for a successful collaborative effort? Do you have to feel passionately about something?*

Mary Jane Stanchina: Absolutely. If there's no passion—if there's no emotional commitment, I don't think the opportunities for a collaborative environment work very well. This relates to the example about the grant; the writers had a commitment to the cause!

> **"If there's no passion—if there's no emotional commitment, I don't think the opportunities for a collaborative environment work very well."**
> —Mary Jane Stanchina

Throughout my professional career in collaborative ventures, working with multiple school districts in multiple counties, I learned that getting to know the "actors" is a great beginning point. It's about learning about the people you are working with. Are they left handed/right handed? What do they value? What makes them tick?

Interviewer: How do you get to know people at that level? Do you take them to dinner?

Mary Jane Stanchina: Social events are highly effective avenues to learn about people; observing people in various professional venues is insightful.

When we get a new superintendent in our Compact, my concern is not about how many degrees he or she has; my concern is, "Can the person share?"

Interviewer: What does that mean?

Mary Jane Stanchina: If you cannot share or give, you have a very difficult time being collaborative. If people are highly autonomous, if they think only about what is good for me and what is good for my school district, it is hard to collaborate.

"Share" means that you're willing to work with others to move forward a cause, a project, or a program.

Interviewer: What characteristics does one who shares have?

Mary Jane Stanchina: A willingness to listen. Listening is an extraordinary skillful talent and is also very intuitive.

Listening is the art of "being present" to what someone else is saying, and that includes an understanding of the language that is used.

> **"Listening is the art of 'being present' to what someone else is saying."**
> **—Mary Jane Stanchina**

We all use different terms, words. We do not always have the same interpretation of what those words mean. Listening is also paying attention and being focused on what one is saying.

In addition to listening and sharing, commitment—having the passion and emotional connectedness—is part of being collaborative.

Trust is another huge element. Our Compact has been in existence for 46 years. There's an understanding and recognition of the history that is meaningful.

We have many administrators who go from one school district to the next for administrative-type positions; they take with them their knowledge of one's own school district as well as five other school districts because they've been engaged in conversations with others through the Compact structure. It is expected that we do our best to work together.

Interviewer: *What are the keys to communicating effectively with others involved in an active collaborative effort?*

Mary Jane Stanchina: First of all, people need to know why they are being collaborative. Every day we work in a collaborate structure within the Six District Educational Compact. It is a way of doing business!

When you're thinking about a project or a special need that exists, then it is helpful for everybody to understand the purpose and why we're moving in that direction. What are the roles and responsibilities going to be of people working in that collaborative? And what is the timeline?

If people come prepared, if they come ready to commit, if they come ready to listen, if they come ready to be engaged and what I call to "be present in the moment," then I believe collaboration on projects is much more effective.

> **"If they come ready to listen, if they come ready to be engaged and what I call to 'be present in the moment,' then I believe collaboration on projects is much more effective."**
> —Mary Jane Stanchina

Knowing the skills of the people involved is important. Some are visual learners, some are global thinkers, some are more attuned to the details, and some are more auditory. Knowing this information is part of the background of working with people and determining how they can contribute to the cause.

The question is, "Why would six school districts do the same project six different ways?" It's ridiculous. By coming together and through the Compact where we have a representative from each school district to address that project or that program, then you get a cross-cultural approach to how we might want to develop this project.

It also has to deal with the concept of "group-think." I've always felt that group-think is far better than single-think because you have the opportunity to obtain a very diverse viewpoint.

> **"I've always felt that group-think is far better than single-think."**
> —Mary Jane Stanchina

Interviewer: When you've seen collaborations fail, why do you think they fail?

Mary Jane Stanchina: They fail because the developers and the facilitators perhaps don't understand the common community of purpose, who the actors are sitting at the table, and the work at hand.

There are people who deliberately try to be disruptive, and when you try to jinx the project or the work, it's most sad. Fortunately, I've not had to deal with many of those situations in my career.

I always liked this quote from Helen Keller, and it goes something like, "Alone we can do so little, but together we can do so much."

That's one of the things that I talk a lot about. I often paraphrase that lovely quote of hers because I think that's exactly what the focus and the target need to be.

> "I often paraphrase Helen Keller's lovely quote, 'Alone we can do so little, but together we can do so much.'"
>
> —Mary Jane Stanchina

Interviewer: What additional thoughts on collaboration would you like to share?

Mary Jane Stanchina: I would like to expand on the issue of trust and relationship building.

Interviewer's Note: Mary Jane here explained a story where she invited a newly-elected state school board member to meet with members of her Compact, and how pleased that new state school board member was with the experience. The state school board member even invited other state school board members to attend. Mary Jane provided this as an example of how reaching out to others on a proactive basis can be highly effective.

Mary Jane Stanchina: State school board members meet with school district personnel frequently. However, we provided them with a unique opportunity of meeting with the six Compact superintendents and the Compact executive director.

They had never been in a Compact setting, so they were interested in learning more about it.

The board members realized that these six superintendents were the autonomous executives of a school district, that they have unique operating styles and skill sets. However, they are also part of another entity that requires trust, humor, and commitment to guide a collaborative entity. They experienced that first hand at this meeting.

This meeting "happened" because a personal/professional friend of over 40 years is a newly appointed state school board member. Since he is a retired college dean and provost, he is a great "fit" for this role. At a social event we discussed his visiting with the Compact superintendents; from there it evolved and happened. It was all about networking and asking for the opportunity.

You have to pay attention and use the relationships you've had in your past and your life to maneuver things.

I don't have any problems asking anybody about anything because you get three answers: yes, no, or maybe.

That's been one of the successes I've had in my career with the collaborative viewpoint. You just ask.

LOWELL W. GERSON, PhD

Lowell Gerson, PhD is professor emeritus of Family and Community Medicine, Northeast Ohio Medical University and senior scientist, Department of Emergency Medicine, Summa Health System-Akron. He is a senior associate editor of *Academic Emergency Medicine* and a member of the MEDICC editorial board. Dr. Gerson chaired the Society for Academic Emergency Medicine (SAEM) Geriatric Task Force. He is considered to have been influential in the development of geriatric emergency medicine. His list of publications speaks to his career of collaboration.

Interviewer: *What are some of your thoughts about collaboration?*

Lowell Gerson: I want to draw a distinction between collaboration and cooperation, where collaboration is a group of folks with different skills coming together in teams to achieve a common goal that benefits everybody in the group. A lot of the projects that I have worked on require collaboration because the problem or the issue was multi-faceted, and you just need people with different skills coming together to find a solution. Most of what I've done collaboratively has been multidisciplinary research project design and execution.

> "Collaboration is a group of folks with different skills coming together in teams to achieve a common goal that benefits everybody in the group."
> —Dr. Lowell W. Gerson

Cooperation I think of as people who are basically serving a more or less selfish interest who will join forces with some other group of individuals. I'm using *selfish*, not in a bad way, but in the sense of individuals who require the assistance of another person to accomplish a task, which is theirs. I've participated, again using the research example where you or your department just does one thing to help somebody else accomplish their complex project, like assisting with data analysis. So you're not really part of the whole picture of recruiting patients or providing clinical interventions, for example.

Interviewer: So you're talking about cooperation versus collaboration.

Lowell Gerson: Right. Cooperation is you're working with somebody but really just to accomplish their ends rather than a group end, if you will—meaning that you might be paid to cooperate.

Interviewer: Actually, we don't cover cooperation in the book at all, nor do we define the differences between collaboration and cooperation. The book pretty much focuses on the process of collaboration and people's various perspectives on that process.

People really discuss ideas that can help make it more successful, explanations of challenges, and what some of the solutions are that can be implemented and get you past those challenges—those kinds of things.

Lowell Gerson: Well, one of the challenges might be what I was just describing, where somebody is thinking of collaboration, but they're really not collaborating. They participate because they're getting something out of it, but they're really not contributing to the overall good.

Interviewer: What would you do if you were in a situation like that?

Lowell Gerson: That's a tough question, of course. We've experienced things like that where we thought we would do a collaboration, and one of the parties was really acting in their own self-interest and eventually dropped out. How much has Bill talked to you about the development of the state wide MPH public health program?

Interviewer: In great detail, as have others in interviews.

Lowell Gerson: Okay, well there were two parties in that collaboration effort who actually kind of withdrew from it and went off on their own, so they weren't really collaborators.

Interviewer: That's an interesting observation. Of course, Bill didn't phrase it that way. He phrased it that they had their own concerns which he respected, and he had told them, "If you don't want to be doing this, feel free to do your own thing." But your perspective is a little different, and what you're saying is that you don't think they were really collaborating at all.

Lowell Gerson: No, I don't think they were collaborating at all. Bill's response is the right one. I mean that was what turned out. They went along, and then, as Bill said, "If you want to go do your own thing, go do it."

Interviewer: Do you see that as a strategy that would likely be successful?

Lowell Gerson: It can be successful, but it wasn't in this case.

Interviewer: *What do you do when the people who are in a collaboration really aren't collaborating? They're pursuing their own selfish interests at the same time that they're working with the collaboration, and at a moment's notice, they will drop it and do their own thing. It seems in Bill's mind that was totally acceptable because he just wanted to make sure there were more MPH programs in the state, and whether it got done through the collaboration or through some other way, at least it was getting done.*

Lowell Gerson: That's correct—except for the effort that was expended that could have been directed elsewhere.

Interviewer: *Bill would probably say that time investment was valuable because they ended up doing their own program and that served the greater good. That time investment helped to provide more MPH programs in the State.*

However, I would say that less than half the people who went through that experience would describe it in as positive a manner [as Bill did].

Lowell Gerson: Yes, probably a lot less than half. But you also raised the point, "What was the goal?" If the goal was to produce more MPHs in Ohio, then that solution is perfect. If the goal was to have strength in having a joint MPH program, then that's a rationalization.

Interviewer: *Well, what do you think the goal was? You were there.*

Lowell Gerson: I thought that the goal was to produce a joint MPH program that could draw on the strengths of everybody within the consortium because the individual schools didn't necessarily have all the resources required for a well-rounded MPH program.

I think we could have had a stronger MPH program that would have required less recruiting of new people and would have saved cash had it been a joint program.

Interviewer: *Another corollary thought is that the challenge of keeping the collaboration going has been an ongoing concern, as one after the other drop out. It's got to be tough to keep going when you know you're going to lose half.*

But that problem has happened over and over again, and what you're saying can have lot of value because it can say to a reader, "What do you really want?" If what you really want is the collaboration—and by that I mean the dynamic of the collaboration, people working together for a common goal—that's one thing.

But if what you want is an end result, then in some instances you might be a little happier with what happens. My guess is that you have more than one story about how collaborations fell apart.

Lowell Gerson: Yes. Well, while I wouldn't say it's fallen apart, the development of geriatric emergency medicine, which I was involved with from the beginning, might be an example. Right now, it's much stronger and growing, so it definitely didn't fall apart [But there were challenges in the past].

Back in the 1980s some recognized that older patients in emergency departments [ED] are not the same as middle-aged patients. They have different needs, their presentation in the ED is different, and their biology is different. This was just beginning to be appreciated at that time.

I happened to have been working with the Akron Emergency Medical System, helping with the evaluation of that new program. I made some observations about older patients' disproportionate use of the EMS system. This lead to my becoming involved in the Society for Geriatric Medicine Geriatric Task Force that was funded by the John A. Hartford Foundation.

The task force brought together people who had really no common appreciation of the need to develop this particular area. None of them had been from geriatric emergency medicine, as there was no such thing identified. They came from different emergency medicine specialty areas: cardiologists, general emergency physicians, pediatric emergency physicians, and me. I got involved because of my research background.

We began with a bunch of studies that characterized the field. This was continued because of an outside force—again the John A. Hartford Foundation—which recognized that there'd never be enough geriatricians and provided funding to come up with a plan to give some special geriatric skills to people in other medical specialties. Folks became involved because they could enhance their own careers, and they appreciated that this was a new, important area that was developing.

Over time, with that core group of people, we influenced many of our colleagues to look at geriatric emergency medicine issues. It created a nice cadre that was now working in that area doing research, developing new skills, and teaching.

The fragmentation began to occur when a few hospitals decided that they could actually characterize their emergency department as a geriatric emergency department. This was more a marketing device than a clear description of competence because there were no standards for making such a claim.

Nevertheless, the people who really were dedicated to improving the practice recognized that a true geriatric emergency department would likely improve care and outcomes of older patients. So this awareness led to a collaboration of a group of people who started to put together an inventory of competencies that one would need to practice geriatric emergency medicine and standards for what would be needed to be called a geriatric emergency department. The outliers produced a collaboration of people who improved the quality of the field by developing competencies and standards.

So sometimes having the outlier influences the main group to produce a better product.

Interviewer: *Would you say that you are personally cautious entering collaborations?*

Lowell Gerson: No, I am not cautious when I enter collaborations. Since beginning my academic career, I realized that the problems I am working with are usually greater than my skills can handle.

> **"I realized that the problems I am working with are usually greater than my skills can handle."**
> —Dr. Lowell W. Gerson

My first big grant was a service delivery model for home care instead of hospital care, and this required a true collaboration between a health economist, a surgeon, a social worker, and me, and then the cooperation of the nursing staff at the hospital to get the information that we needed.

The nurses cooperated because there was a payoff for them, in that they got to better understand what they were actually accomplishing regarding care and how they could best divide their time between basic and technical care. They recognized the outcome of the project could help them in their daily work.

So I've always tried to push collaborations, and if you look at what I've done, it's almost all been collaborative.

I'm not skilled enough to do anything by myself.

Interviewer: *Is there anything else you'd like to mention about collaboration?*

Lowell Gerson: My bottom line is that most problems are pretty complex and require a variety of skills to deal with them.

You need to establish a shared goal of improving whatever you want to improve. And one of the other things is that in a collaboration you have to be willing to accept what the other people on the team say because of their special skills, knowledge, and experiences.

That's how I've tried to operate.

FREDERICA L. COHEN

Frederica Cohen was a music educator of strings in the Akron and Cuyahoga Falls City School Districts for 28 years. She was the founding director/teacher of The New Horizons Orchestra of Summit and Stark Counties for 10 years and is a co-author of *Love Of Chromatic Harmonica Techniques And Advice from the World's Best!*

Interviewer: *Tell me a little bit about collaboration.*

Frederica Cohen: Collaboration—I think your success depends upon how well you actually learned it as you grew up. It's a skill that you have to acquire as you grow. And if you're always in the position of being "right" all the time—and need to be right all the time—you're not going to be a successful collaborator.

You have to learn to give and take as you go.

"You have to learn to give and take as you go."
—Frederica Cohen

Interviewer: *Do you think that you define it that way because you were a strings teacher in the public school system?*

Frederica Cohen: That's a possibility, but I think everybody needs to learn give and take no matter what, no matter where you are in life.

Interviewer: *How would you help a student who didn't know much about collaboration understand it?*

Frederica Cohen: I tried to get them all to realize that as part of an orchestra you had a place, and it took everybody to make the piece successful. Everything was important, and it had to all work together, or we didn't have a successful piece at the end.

Interviewer: *So you defined their role for them and their importance in the big picture.*

Frederica Cohen: Even with my adults, when we started to actually do pieces, I had to make the violins understand that the 2nd violin part was just as important as the 1st violin, because without it, we didn't really have all the parts that were necessary.

Interviewer: *You had situations where you would work with another organization—with the school collaborating on something. Tell me about one of those experiences.*

Frederica Cohen: It was an interesting experience because the collaboration was set up without all the parties being consulted, and that created a rather disjointed affair.

> "The collaboration was set up without all the parties being consulted, and that created a rather disjointed affair."
>
> —Frederica Cohen

Interviewer: *Explain that a little.*

Frederica Cohen: Well, there was a program set up for after-school enrichment activities, and every department was asked to submit ideas for what would be good for their department. The music department submitted the idea of private lessons for the students given by professionals with The Akron Symphony who would come to the school. It actually came about.

But we weren't asked to submit the finite ideas and the best way to go carry them out; we were just asked to submit the big idea. We did. They never came back to us and consulted us on the best way that things might work or how to work with the organization that actually did this.

So we were presented with a program that had some flaws in the long run, but we had no way of working them out. And those flaws made for some disjointedness, which actually created some bad feelings between the community and the organization that was giving the private lessons.

Interviewer: *What was the nature of that conflict?*

Frederica Cohen: They would take all the students who wanted to show up for the first few sessions, but the materials describing the program indicated that if you made it to all those sessions, you would get private lessons. But only 10 to 12 children were actually selected for private lessons, and there was no indication in the materials that were sent out originally that that was the case.

The parents were very angry and said, "Well, my child made it to every single session. Why aren't they getting private lessons? That's what the material says." But the people who created the materials weren't there to explain it, and that left me as the moderator having to explain what was going on, and I really didn't have the answers.

Interviewer: So there was lack of shared expectation. Parents thought if the kids went to every group lesson/rehearsal, they'd get private lessons, but in reality only 10-12 got private lessons.

Frederica Cohen: There were also issues with the private teacher not showing up and not notifying anybody. Or the child was absent.

The expectations of how all these things were to be done were never shared with anybody—and it left a rather nasty taste in the mouth. I was to be paid a certain amount of money for staying after school and watching things because children were not supposed to be in the building without a state certified teacher, and I had to stay until the children were picked up. A lot of these children were there after the "activity bus" had left, and I could not leave until all these teachers had left the building as well.

I was told, "Well, you're getting too much money."

I responded, "Well, I can't leave. My job description says the children have to be gone; then the teachers need to be gone.

Interviewer: So it sounds like the details were not well organized.

Frederica Cohen: Right. And when I went to meet with people at the orchestra about this and suggested a change in how they presented the materials, that wasn't well received.

Interviewer: What happened?

Frederica Cohen: I said, "You know, you're stating that if you come to the first four sessions, you will receive private lessons, but that is not the fact. The fact is you're only going to select 10 to 12 children on your criteria, which is never really stated. We teachers don't even really know what your criteria are. You're creating a bad feeling in the community around the school. Why don't you state it a little differently?

Interviewer: How did they respond when you brought these concerns to their attention?

Frederica Cohen: They argued with me, they didn't choose to change it, and I was in no position to be able to do anything because I was only the school's representative, not the person in charge of the after-school program.

Interviewer: Do you think there were shared goals in this instance?

Frederica Cohen: No, because no one ever asked us as the music department what our goal was.

Interviewer: What would your goal have been?

Frederica Cohen: Our goal would have been that if only that small number of children participated, let us choose the children that would have received the lessons—those who would have benefited the most from these lessons—as opposed to you randomly picking these kids. Some of these kids would take a couple of lessons and quit, and that would be the end of it because they didn't want to do the work.

Interviewer: They didn't know the kids.

Frederica Cohen: They didn't know the kids; we did.

Interviewer: How many children participated in the program total?

Frederica Cohen: 30 to 40 children came to the first few sessions, but only 25 children attended all four sessions. Then only half of them—or fewer—were picked for lessons that continued for an academic year.

Interviewer: So this is obviously a story of a collaboration that in some respects was a failure.

Frederica Cohen: There was only one real positive story that came out of that: a child with a learning disability was able to study French horn.

Interviewer: How would you have organized all this if you had been in charge of the whole thing?

Frederica Cohen: I would have preferred that the person who was in charge of the whole program at the school come to those of us in the music department and ask us what we wanted to see, and not just have gone and set up a program. I think there would have been a better chance to have a much more successful program.

Interviewer: So if it's insular—if the person putting together the program doesn't get input from the people doing the work—the chances for success are much less?

Frederica Cohen: It would seem that way, for sure. Because if you set up a program without input from the people who are going to have to run it, especially if you have no knowledge in that area, the chances of success are much slimmer.

> "If you set up a program without input from the people who are going to have to run it . . . the chances of success are much slimmer."
>
> —Frederica Cohen

The program existed for about three years, and the issues were ongoing the whole time.

We were never told why the program was shut down.

ARDITH KECK

Ardith Keck has her BA in romance languages, English, and history, and, now retired, taught Spanish at the junior as well as senior high school level. She is also a host and chair of a thirty-minute interview show, *Forum 360*, on PBS TV, WONE and WAKR radio in Akron. She has also organized and moderated League of Women Voters candidates' forums for TV and radio. Ardith founded and served as president of River Run Arts-Earth Studies Camp Inc. The camp is now run by the Cuyahoga Valley National Park.

Interviewer: How do you feel about the idea of a book on collaboration?

Ardith Keck: Well, it's certainly a worthwhile topic, and I believe in collaboration. I obviously like to have my husband promoted in terms of what he has done, so that makes sense. I think collaboration is one of the best parts of any relationship, and therefore, yes, I think it's great.

Interviewer: Do you think of marriage as collaboration?

Ardith Keck: Absolutely. It's a partnership and it requires a lot of collaboration because if you don't do that, you "ain't" got a marriage. There are a lot of people who are married, but maybe they don't collaborate together—work together—because working together is collaboration. If you don't work together, it's not much of a marriage.

> **"Working together is a collaboration. If you don't work together, it's not much of a marriage."**
> —Ardith Keck

Interviewer: What's your read on the challenges that Bill faced in some of his collaborations in terms of what he went through as a human being—his feelings? It's not an organizational question. What did he have to go through emotionally to survive?

Ardith Keck: He's a person who is pretty even-tempered and deals with people very evenly, so there were times when I—I who am more fiery and not as easy going a person as he is—wanted him to be more fiery because I wanted him to get his way, as far as who he was collaborating with.

Interviewer: What makes Bill a good collaborator?

Ardith Keck: I think a lot of people would say, and I would say, that he doesn't live by his ego. He does not have a big ego. He does not think he's as wonderful as he is. He can do what's best for the group, rather than do what's best for him. Bill works well with people; he's easy to deal with, and this goes along with his lack of fiery attitude. It's very helpful in collaboration to be able to work from another's viewpoint, which he does very well.

Interviewer: *What can you tell me about what it takes to see things from another person's viewpoint?*

Ardith Keck: You can't be a dominating person. You can't be someone whose ego is so large that you know you're right and that's the only way there is. You have to see things in a group way, or see things in an all-inclusive way.

Interviewer: *Do you think that was one of the reasons you were drawn to him in your personal relationship?*

Ardith Keck: Probably, although when we started our relationship, he was pretty shy.

Interviewer: *What else makes him a good collaborator?*

Ardith Keck: I guess I would say that if you are willing to listen to other viewpoints and make your goals their goals or have joint goals, it works well. You can't collaborate without having the same goals.

Interviewer: *How would you describe Bill's approach to communication?*

Ardith Keck: That has changed a lot, but right now, I would say Bill's approach to communication is excellent. He listens and understands people, and he does not dominate people.

Interviewer: *How would you define "listening?"*

Ardith Keck: Actually hearing what people say, not just sitting there and saying, "Umh hmmm, Umh humm, right," but actually hearing it and maybe changing your viewpoint to go along with what they're saying.

Interviewer: You have been successful at collaborative efforts in your own right. What you would say to a group of people listening to you speak on the topic of collaboration?

Ardith Keck: Well, collaboration is working together, and if you want to achieve your goal, the best way to do it just about in every sense—just about always—is to collaborate. Very few times can you achieve as much by yourself as you can in collaboration with others.

> **"Very few times can you achieve as much by yourself as you can in collaboration with others."**
> —Ardith Keck

Your goal should be to work together and maybe to find a way to get around the reasons why it might not work. That means change what you're thinking, change where you are, and change how you want to do things.

Interviewer: What do you think the impediments to successful collaboration are?

Ardith Keck: Lack of interest. The League of Women Voters has found that in some of our collaborations, people agreed to collaborate, but there really wasn't the interest there, so nothing happened. It became clear over time, when the actual workload was only done by the League of Women Voters. No one else showed up to help.

Interviewer: Some of the stories that Bill has told about collaboration involve early goals not being able to be met—for example, consolidation of independent health departments—and yet he went on to collaborate and eventually got consolidation. What is the correct approach when you hit a logjam in collaboration? What is the correct response when you hit a brick wall?

Ardith Keck: Try and try again. I think there have been many unsuccessful collaborations just because people gave up. I don't give up easily, and a lot of people don't give up easily. Bill certainly doesn't. If you are able to work through people's objections, or their problems with collaboration, or their lack of interest in collaboration, you just might get them eventually—if you work at it.

Interviewer: What is the most advantageous mindset for someone who wants to engage in collaboration?

Ardith Keck: Probably the most advantageous mindset is listening and attempting to make sure other's views are understood. Maybe you're going to change to their views and maybe not, but it certainly behooves you to sit down and say, "What is it you want?"

Interviewer: What do you see as the application or utility of a book that delves into collaboration?

Ardith Keck: I think what we're trying to do by explaining collaboration in its many forms and many ways to do it is the correct approach, because anyone who's trying to collaborate and not succeeding needs a little bit of help in putting a plan together to try to make it successful.

I actually think that a book like this, which is not as specific as a textbook but includes stories, can help even those who are working to collaborate on a TV show, to collaborate in the League of Women Voters, or in other organizations—even a singing group. Hopefully, there will be methods and hints—special little ideas—that come forth in the book that you wouldn't have heard everywhere else.

Interviewer: Would you say that Bill is an unusually effective collaborator? Where would you rank him on a 0-10 scale on his collaboration skills?

Ardith Keck: I would say he's probably a ten, knowing that those who worked for him called him "the velvet hammer" because he could deal with tense situations in a very gentle way. That's pretty much his way.

Interviewer: Do you believe that effectiveness in collaboration leadership is related to the age of the individual who's leading the collaboration effort?

Ardith Keck: I don't believe there's a ratio of importance with age. I think it deals more with ego and knowing where you want to go and how you want to get there.

Interviewer: If you look at your own personality—you're not Bill; you're Ardith—what issues do you personally face with collaboration?

Ardith Keck: Well, I'm always right [laughs], and that makes collaboration more difficult sometimes. I think one of the similarities between Bill and me relating to collaboration is that our egos don't get in the way of understanding what other people need.

There's always the challenge of other people not understanding where you need to get to eventually. You can see it very clearly, but you may not be able to get others to face that or realize that.

Interviewer: Do you think American society today makes collaboration more, or less difficult?

Ardith Keck: I doubt that collaboration has changed a lot in this society over the years. I can think back to when I was younger and attempted collaborations and when Bill was younger and attempted them. I'm not sure much has changed over the years.

BILL'S COMMENTARY ON ARDITH'S INTERVIEW

Bill Keck: Discussing things between us is one of the ways we help each other decide what the right approach is to deal with a collaboration problem. I think each of us has managed to alter the course that the other was taking in some circumstances, but those discussions can be difficult.

Ardith's or my pointing out to the other some alternative ways around a problem can get us thinking more broadly. For example, Ardith can say to me, "There's a time to be mild and inclusive, and sometimes there's a time to be a little bit more forceful and to push the issue."

In some of the playoff we've had over the years, each of us gives advice to the other and then steps back, saying, "It's your decision, you need to go with it." You're the one living in that environment; you're the one that knows the other personalities. We just talk about options and different approaches and then step back, and whichever one of us is moving ahead with it does so pretty much on their own. It doesn't mean we won't come back and talk about it again, however.

That sort of playing off each other helps, and I think it helps that we're not exactly alike in how we look at things.

Ardith Keck: I think that helps a marriage a lot, if you're not too identical.

Bill Keck: So far we've been able to do this. Nobody has ended up crying in the bathroom, right?

Ardith Keck: Oh yes, early on. We weren't the same people early on, however.

[Both laugh.]

NARRATIVES

Narratives are a series of stories from Dr. Keck's career that give a feel for the true give-and-take, frustrations, and—at times—success which accompany activities in collaboration.

You are the best judge of what each section "teaches," if teaching is the right word.

NARRATIVE #1

THE MAKING OF A FIRE DEPARTMENT-BASED EMERGENCY MEDICAL SYSTEM

Bill Keck: In 1978, the Akron Fire Department took an ordinance to City Council, which passed, creating a fire department-based emergency medical system. I did not know that the legislation had been submitted. I had been told that such legislation was under consideration and had expressed an opinion that was sort of negative, feeling that the fire department didn't have the necessary resources. But they didn't pay any attention to that, and that was probably the right thing to do.

Then I woke up one morning to read in the newspaper that this ordinance had passed and that part of it was the formation of an Emergency Medical Services Advisory Board to the mayor and that the chair was the director of health—which happened to be me.

So I woke up to a fait accompli.

After I adjusted my feelings to being blindsided, I decided I had to get involved and make it work. And in order to make it work, we had to have a collaborative relationship between the fire department, private ambulance companies, and the four hospitals in town. The hospitals were represented by physicians who were the chairs of the hospitals' departments of emergency medicine.

We had a very disparate set of partners.

And somehow we had to make all this work, in terms of the fire department transporting life and limb threatening emergencies at no charge, but all other transports would go to private companies who would charge for their services.

And then the question was how would this be organized and managed from a medical perspective, since the core of the medical expertise existed in the emergency departments in the three adult hospitals that were then operating in Akron and a children's hospital.

So, with those four hospitals involved, the question was which one (and it had to be one) would be the medical control—the place that would provide medical backup for the paramedics and the place that would be called when paramedics confronted a patient who needed something beyond basic primary care or a bandage.

Suddenly we were in a very strict, difficult contest between the chairs of the emergency departments in the hospitals. This got to the point in our monthly meetings where physicians argued publicly with each other about which hospital was more qualified to be medical control and attain the status that came with that designation. Our meetings were open to the public and usually attended by the press, since this was a major story at the time because it indicated a huge change in services available in Akron. It got to the point where passions became a bit heated, and these folks began to call each other names and suggest that their colleagues weren't competent. I believed this was counterproductive and shouldn't have been aired publicly.

One person in particular, one of the emergency department chairs, was particularly irascible and difficult in these conversations.

So I arranged a subcommittee to discuss this—the usual bureaucratic approach, right? I brought in my epidemiologist friend, Dr. Lowell Gerson, from the medical school to be the scientific arbitrator. There was data available on some of the issues we were discussing on who was best qualified and what was best for a patient that would help us make those decisions. This group agreed that Dr. Gerson's credentials were good and that they would follow his lead on what was scientifically appropriate.

By getting this group into a separate venue with an outside arbitrator, we were able to hash this through point by point, largely out of the public view.

It was not easy. If memory serves, it took us 5-6 months to eventually come to a decision, and that decision was forced by deadlines that were built into the legislation. The law specified a certain time when the system was supposed to be up and operational and all the pieces and parts in place. Everybody finally agreed to the parameters the day before the deadline, but we got it done.

Once that agreement was struck, the people who had been fighting each other and had been particularly difficult for me to deal with began to change and slipped into their more traditional medical professional role. From that point, we had a fairly collegial relationship. That was very helpful because we had a lot of remaining legal, medical, organizational, and financial issues to deal with as the system became operational.

What finally settled the medical control issue was board certification for the specialty of emergency medicine. This was in the very early days of board certification for emergency medicine, and it turns out there was only one hospital that had a chairman who was board-certified. He was one of the first in the country. And that became the hook on which we hung the decision. Of course, within a few years, everybody was board-certified, but at that point, it allowed us to make a choice. So Akron General Medical Center became the medical control for the city's EMS system. And as far as I know, they still are.

Interviewer: *What is the lesson from this narrative?*

Bill Keck: Here, we were dealing with relatively high-level professionals who were confronting issues of ego and position not only for themselves but also for their institutions. The trick was to move the discussion away from the personal and closer to the professional. For me, it meant thinking very carefully about what was bringing the most heat to our discussions and finding ways to help resolve the conflicts that existed in a way that would save face and produce results that would be accepted by all of the participants.

The key elements were moving the venue to a less public forum, bringing in a respected third party person who could help appeal to the "scientist" that was part of all the physicians involved, and eventually finding the distinguishing factor(s) that would allow us to make a choice of medical control hospital that would be generally accepted.

NARRATIVE #2

ADDRESSING HIV: UNUSUAL SOLUTIONS AND UNUSUAL PERSPECTIVES

Bill Keck: The HIV epidemic began in the early 80s, and as you know, it took a number of years for people to respond to it. The fear was high, the fear mongering was high, and coordination was poor. There were many unknowns related to what HIV was, how it was transmitted, and how it could be treated.

As the 80s moved along and the epidemiology was worked out, we began to understand what it was, and we finally were able to get the Reagan administration to say the words and respond to it. Federal funding began to ratchet up, and there was also some support at the state level.

The concern then became what do we do at the local level to try to better deal with HIV, and we had to deal with it from a number of perspectives. The Akron Health Department obviously was involved in public education about its epidemiology and how to prevent its spread.

But then we began to see an expansion of this cohort of HIV patients that needed medical services, social services, and other kinds of support such as counseling and housing. And a number of people—many of them from the gay community—began to step forward, saying, "I want to be involved in trying to deal with this."

This was a gutsy move on the part of many of them because the risk of being closely associated with HIV patients still wasn't really understood, but the fact that these patients really needed care, help, and support was motivational. Caring members of the community came together to provide whatever assistance they could.

But then we began to get into the situation where there was growing competition for the available funds. We had all these different issues requiring attention, and small not-for-profit organizations began to form to address them.

One group looked principally at housing. Where would these people stay? They were being discriminated against in housing, particularly those that were ill and not able to take care of themselves fully. Where could they go? Who would support them?

In addition there were legal and medical needs, and social services like food and counseling. It wasn't long however, before these new organizations began to compete with each other for funding and enter an area of conflict.

We were watching this at the health department, where we were tasked with coordinating applications for federal and state funding that was all funneled through the state health department for the three or four groups who were active in HIV-related services. As time passed the competitive conflicts began to increase, particularly as the funding peaked, stabilized, and then began to diminish.

So now we had a lot of people making their living from HIV as well as dying from it. The fights between them became bitter, and the willingness to collaborate began to disappear.

The question that confronted us at the health department was, "Is there anything we can do to resolve these issues instead of just letting these groups form individually and then ply their trade among the needy population? Should we do something to try to maximize the gain and minimize the conflict?"

I decided that I would take on the role of trying to coordinate this group and communicate with them. I had some leverage with all of them, so I said, "The fighting has to stop. We need to come together, determine what everybody's role is, and support each other." I wanted to make sure the patients got served well and to try to make sure that the funders weren't turned off by the internecine warfare that was beginning to break out among these agencies.

We formed an HIV coordination group and held regular meetings that I called and chaired. We essentially went through what the needs of the HIV community were, what the needs of the general community were in terms of education, and who was responsible for what. We were successful to the degree that all the essential services were now available and better linked.

Some of the individuals involved didn't necessarily love each other after that, but they understood that if they didn't work together well, then they wouldn't have health department support, which would be a negative for them in terms of continuation of funding. I used that leverage to bring them together. Then we tried to create an environment where everybody won and where they were more likely to have success with less conflict if they played the game.

That worked quite well actually and went on as long as I was at the health department.

Interviewer: *How did you encourage these folks to get along?*

Bill Keck: First, I had a relationship with all of them, so I was one of several common denominators among them. But I was also the one from the health department whose support they needed to make their funding applications realistic.

The threat of withholding that support was certainly one important factor. Maybe it's just my personality too, since I had worked with all of them, and since I was willing to work with them.

Interviewer: *How do you do that? Assume I'm on the housing side and there's been a disagreement with someone on the medical side.*

Bill Keck: I would generally come back to the basic purpose—many of these folks were from the gay community; they felt this infection personally, and many of them had been personally touched by it. At least one of them who was involved claimed to be HIV positive.

They had friends, colleagues, and lovers who were sick and dying, and this was early in the epidemic before effective treatments were available. An HIV diagnosis was pretty much a death sentence, and it was a difficult environment, watching people deteriorate in front of you and die knowing there's not a damn thing you can do except try to keep them comfortable. It was almost like running a hospice.

But because of the discrimination and fear that existed in the community toward anybody who carried that diagnosis, there was a unifying factor that our job was to make life as pleasant and tolerable for these people as we could.

So I would come back to the idea that when we argued like this the communication between us was hindered.

Interviewer: *This is logical. You just presented the argument for working together.*

Bill Keck: Our stated purpose was serving these folks. We couldn't serve them well if we were not dealing well with each other.

I put the health department's reputation on the line, saying, "I will support you, I'll do what I can in the community. I will help mediate if necessary."

We created an environment—a culture almost, I guess—where continuing the old arguments took place outside the culture. Then the culture was we had to work through our differences and manage those scarce resources well.

Interviewer: *Do you think the outcome would have been the same if you hadn't had control of the purse strings?*

Bill Keck: Well, I didn't really have control of the purse strings; I guess I had influence. There's no question that was a factor.

There were other issues that complicated our work. For example, the HIV epidemic disproportionately affected—and continues to affect—people of color. Why?

There are several reasons: more IV drug use perhaps and more maternal/child transmission. Also, homosexuality was more closeted, so people tended not to protect themselves well because they didn't want to admit they were gay or were having relations with a sex that matched theirs.

But much of it was wrapped up in the black culture, and we couldn't find black leaders in the community that would help us.

One of the major social institutions in the black community is the church, the black churches. Black ministers are a fairly conservative lot in general and railed against the sins of homosexuality. It was very difficult for them to come to grips with the fact that that may very well help spread the infection in their community.

And I didn't know what to do about that. While I had the sort of power that goes with the director of health position, I wasn't at all sure I was in a position to talk directly to the black community and be taken seriously.

So I asked one or two prominent black leaders in town to help me with this and to call together a group of people who could advise me. There was a former public health nurse who is now quite prominent in the black community. She left the health department, got a Doctoral degree, directed a few major organizations in town, and had good academic connections. I knew her fairly well and said, "Help me identify major players in the black community." With her help we identified a few black councilmen, key black ministers, and one or two others, and I asked them to come to a meeting in the health department.

I laid out the data for them, which showed how their community was suffering disproportionately from this. Infection rates were 2-3 times that of whites. And of course, it was largely a city of Akron problem, since there weren't that many black people that lived outside of the city. So I demonstrated the problem for them and said, "You see my concern. That's an important problem for us to find a way to address, and I need your help. How do I do this?"

The result was that I got almost no help at all, which was interesting. I said, "The health department will provide all the support you need to anyone you designate or think should be appropriate here. We'll provide them with the information they need, we'll provide them with backup, we'll get free condoms, we'll do all that we can to support you, but I need a prominent black face out front. Okay? And we'll be right behind you."

So I got lots of discussion but no real volunteers. They promised, however, to think about it and get back to me.

Sadly, that never happened.

After a few follow up inquiries, it was clear they just weren't going to deal with it.

That was a failure.

My former nurse was as disappointed as I was.

Interviewer: *What's the take-away here?*

Bill Keck: The take-away is you can't always win. Maybe I didn't find the right stakeholders. We did have a few black gay men who were prominent in trying to help educate that community, but that wasn't enough.

Interviewer: *Maybe nobody got involved because if they were gay, they didn't want anybody to know they were gay. And if they were straight, they didn't want people to think they were gay because they were fighting for a gay cause. Either way, they weren't going to touch it.*

Bill Keck: If a prominent leader thought about getting involved, I think they calculated that their perceived value in the community would not increase if they suddenly became champions for HIV prevention.

So that was one more where I was seeking collaboration without success.

NARRATIVE #3

COMBINING MULTIPLE AGENCIES INTO ONE—FOR EFFICIENCY AND BETTER CARE OF THE PUBLIC

From Dr. Bill Keck:

Ever since I came to Akron, it seemed to me that public health would be stronger here if we had just one health department in the county rather than three: two city health departments and a county health department.

I tried several times to manage a consolidation, but obviously key to this would be the five members of my Board of Health—people to whom I reported as Akron's health director. I was very straightforward with them about this, helping them understand that if we were ever successful at consolidation, the need for a city board of health would probably disappear. Because state law required consolidated health departments to be a county health department, the organizational structure would change, and the boards of health would have to be merged in some fashion.

Despite that reality we looked for opportunities to go ahead, and there were several through the years when the leaders of the Summit County Health Department retired. I told the board that I would like to pursue the idea, at least, and got their blessing, understanding that it had both positive and perhaps not so positive implications for the Akron Health Department.

The major potential advantages were efficiency of services, representation of a larger population which made us more highly eligible for external funding, better care for patients, better program coordination, services that were more seamless, and less bureaucracy. To their credit, they were on board with those ideas. The negatives, of course, included lots of work to meld three systems and the likely disappearance of the Akron Board of Health.

I told them some of the things I wanted to do to try to make this happen, that I wanted to take advantage of some of these opportunities to push it with the other boards, and that I would need their help to make it work. The result was we became a team with the people I reported to, saying, perhaps it would help to take some of the mysteries of consolidation away if the boards got to know each other personally. We asked the other two boards of health if they would be willing to meet together at least once a year to discuss issues that were common to the county as a whole rather than just their particular geographical area.

The other boards agreed to the idea, and we began to have annual meetings. We rotated the meetings from one health department to another, and we got to the point where many of these folks were on a first-name basis with each other and had a good general understanding of public health activities and needs across the county.

The first time we tried for a vote on consolidation my board voted yes, but the County Board of Health remained several votes shy of joining us in this process, which was a disappointment to both my board and me. I'll confess there was also an element of relief, too, that we didn't have to yet face the whole new work agenda that would be required in a merger.

It was a real combination of relief and disappointment.

Then we said perhaps what we could do was begin to cooperate in ways that would also make it easier to eventually consolidate if we were able to remove some of the existing barriers. So the question was, could we actually do that in a meaningful way? Could we find ways to communicate better, coordinate our activities, and eventually collaborate on service delivery?

And we said well, let's talk about it from the perspective of the patient and what is convenient and best for them. We now have geographic boundaries within which the three of us operate: two cities (Akron and Barberton) and the rest of the county.

We don't necessarily have services available where they are most convenient for people, however. In other words, there might be something in the city of Akron that's close to the border with the county, where it would be more efficient and effective for county folks to be seen, and vice-versa.

When we explored the legality of this, we found there was nothing that prevented us from seeing patients from other jurisdictions. That led us to look at the areas where we could coordinate, and needed to, in terms of efficient and effective service delivery. As I described earlier in the book, that resulted in unified medical policies and our ability to act as one unit in terms of our clinics.

Interviewer: Did you go down that path because you thought it would help overcome resistance or because you thought it was a good thing from a service perspective, no matter what the outcome would be?

Bill Keck: Both. Yes, we thought it would be better for our patients. We thought if we could integrate our services to some degree that our staffs would learn to know and trust each other. If we had the boards of health meeting together at least once a year where we could report to them on these joint activities, we could show them that we could work together and that it would have some positive outcomes.

We thought that reality might eventually make a consolidation decision easier.

We could then also look at infectious disease reporting. I've already described what we did to simplify the reporting of communicable diseases to the health departments and coordinate the public health response to disease threats across the county (See page 65). Our success won us praise from the medical community because it made their lives easier, and the three boards of health received it very well because it affirmed their decision to work together.

Interviewer: And you kind of picked one that didn't have dollars attached. My point is that the test ground wasn't cash oriented. It didn't affect their revenue; I would imagine that reporting disease is not related to money at all.

Bill Keck: Well, it's certainly linked to staff salaries and the budgets of the health departments.

Interviewer: Do you mean that reporting certain diseases increases your revenue stream?

Bill Keck: No, what it means is that you have the staff available to respond, and if we could draw from a combined staff, we would be more efficient, to say the least, and it would mean that we could share skills. A good example of that was our highly qualified public health physician who now had countywide responsibility, not just the city.

It's part of this larger story of trying to get to a health department consolidation, all of us working on ways to make that happen. We were not successful in getting the consolidation so we made the conscious decision to start doing things that pretended we were consolidated where we could.

Interviewer: You could look at it a lot of ways. It was a nice test; it was a way to see what the ground might feel like.

Bill Keck: And it was clearly intended as a prelude to another effort at consolidation. It was a conscious approach that we took to try to smooth the path to combining the three health departments. Later we had another opportunity while I was still health director, and the leader of one of the other health departments retired. It failed again. It was close, but it still didn't quite make it.

So we began to wonder, "Did we nix it by being so good at collaborating? Or was there just too much ego involved in home rule?" Who knows?

My retirement was another opportunity to consolidate, but nobody took it up. Seven or eight years after I retired, however, we were in the middle of the recession that began in 2008. Now people were looking to be more efficient with dollars as local government budgets suffered. Akron's mayor had previously said that he would let the law department look at this, but he didn't understand why I might suggest to him that he should give up all these assets to the county. I told him it would likely lead to more efficient and effective public health services, so he humored me. He said, "Because you are asking, we will quietly look at the legalities here." The mayor did not appoint me, nor did I report to him. He was a key to success in this endeavor, however, so I wanted him to know what this was all about. Even though merger did not occur during my tenure as director of health, his acquiescence to looking at the legalities meant some of the background work for merger was accomplished.

Interviewer: Who did appoint you?

Bill Keck: The board of health. That was one reason I took the job. It wasn't a political appointment. The board of health was made up of five appointees of the mayor.

Interviewer: The hand is there; it's just not a direct hand.

Bill Keck: You couldn't really have it any other way in a political entity. I went out of my way to keep him informed, not nearly to the same degree as the board of health, of course, but because he was a major player in this, I felt it important to avoid surprises and to have the opportunity to answer his questions as the process unfolded. Then later after I retired, when the financial and political stars lined up, he became a strong proponent of health department consolidation and pushed to make it happen. The county executive shared his enthusiasm. Even though the Summit County Health Department did not report directly to the county executive—it was and still is a separate entity—it helped to have the county executive's support.

Interviewer: And so in this case, the county executive is voted on by the public, so you have that individual and the mayor with clout, and they are both independent and happened to be Democrats, so they could afford to have their own views.

Who had the real authority to make the decision?

Bill Keck: The boards of health would have to vote to merge, and the city and county councils would have to both agree and pass legislation to allow merger. The mayor and county executive did not control the health departments, which were set up as independent entities. The whole idea was to keep public health relatively apolitical. That's a smart arrangement, and, as I said, it is one of the reasons I came to Akron in the first place.

This is an example of a long game—an almost 40 year game. But eventually, it came to pass because, I believe, the boards of health worked through their concerns and came to be supportive. The City of Barberton Health Department was not part of the original merger, but the handwriting was on the wall for them. They realized that continuing to exist as a small agency next to a comparative behemoth during a time of diminishing resources did not bode well for them. I don't know the details that led to Barberton's decision to join the merger, but I know eventually the mayor and the board of health came on board and agreed that Barberton should join the merger.

The boards of health agreed to really explore this, the major political figures were on board, and a feasibility committee was put together, chaired by one of the most popular health figures in town, Bill Considine, the chief executive officer of Children's Hospital. This long-time CEO, who is very community and public health-oriented and a trusted leader, agreed to chair this group to explore the political, the organizational, and the financial issues associated with bringing three health departments together. A consensus quickly emerged that this consolidation not only was wise; it was also doable. The committee recommendation was to proceed with the merger, and it went on to happen.

Interviewer: *What are the major lessons you learned from this experience?*

Bill Keck: Retelling all of these stories reminds me how important it is to have a core group of folks with good judgment whom you trust to maintain your confidence, but also to tell you exactly what they're thinking. This is especially important when the circumstances are difficult and complex. Never really believe that you understand everything about the relationships that you're trying to build and the services you're trying to provide.

I can't emphasize enough how important it was for me to be able to bounce ideas back and forth between trusted confidants, knowing they would tell me if they thought I was heading in the wrong direction and would not be loath to suggest something different than what I was proposing. I needed a small group to be very quietly honest with me, and I wanted folks who were used to and comfortable with that kind of exchange.

It can be really helpful in exploring the ramifications of the decisions you're about to make to make sure you are considering the elements that are most important to the decision before you step out in front and move, one way or another.

Interviewer's comment: *This is one of my favorite narratives, as strictly speaking, the combination of health departments never occurred in Dr. Keck's tenure. It happened after he was gone. So many times in life, we may feel we have failed to reach goals, only to find another player runs the ball over the goal line after us.*

Failure can actually be success, and vice-versa!

NARRATIVE #4

IMPROVED TRAINING FOR THE PUBLIC HEALTH WORKFORCE

Bill Keck: When I first came to Akron in the late 1980s, there was only one training program in the state that was related to public health, outside of medicine and dentistry. There was a master's degree in preventive medicine offered at Ohio State University, but there were no other public health degrees available in the state. Meanwhile, I was trying to set up an academic connection that would, among other things, create an educational career path for people who wanted to work in public health, and we had no place in the state to send them to get a master's degree or a doctorate degree.

So I had this idea that maybe since my medical school, the Northeastern Ohio Universities College of Medicine [NEOUCOM]—now the Northeast Ohio Medical University—was interested in public health and pushing to improve training in community health sciences, that maybe there would be similar interest at the six other medical schools in the state. I sat down with my deputy at the medical school, Dr. Lowell Gerson, talked this out, and said, "Could we get all seven medical schools working together collaboratively to essentially produce a statewide school of public health?"

I communicated with the accrediting body for schools of public health to see if that was a model that might fly, and I was told there was nothing quite like that but they would certainly be willing to look. They didn't tell me they couldn't accredit something like that, and didn't say that they would without seeing it, but they encouraged me to pursue it.

Lowell and I decided to move ahead. We did an environmental scan by looking at what the pedagogical and research strengths were at each institution, and we found out there was significant variation. We considered that a strength because if we could bring them together, we would give students the potential to have access to a really wide range of skills and experiences—a much wider range than you get in a smaller program or in a normal stand-alone program or school.

We presented the idea to our counterparts at the six other medical schools and were pleased to get a very positive response. With their encouragement we arranged a first organizational meeting that was quite optimistic, and we all agreed to meet regularly to develop our plan. We met over a period of about two years and were making real progress when the Ohio State University representative announced his institution was going to leave the group and form their own program or school. That discouraged several of our partner institutions that said without Ohio State involvement, they didn't think they could proceed. We could see the early signs of the group disintegrating.

The representative from the Toledo area then said to me, "You know, we'll hold up on moving ahead while we rethink this," and I looked at them and I said, "That's crazy; you should not do that."

Interviewer: What does it mean, "We'll hold up"?

Bill Keck: He told me they were thinking about creating their own consortium MPH program with their medical school and other universities in the Toledo area, but they'd much rather be part of something larger. They offered to slow down that process to see if we could work something out, despite one school and then a second school leaving the group.

And then, of course, the leadership changed at another school at Case Western Reserve. Case decided to back out and go ahead on its own, and I said to the folks from Toledo, "It's not in your best interest to slow down and wait for us. You don't want to put your own consortium at risk because it appears this sort of far out idea isn't going to work." After more discussion Toledo decided it should go ahead on its own.

We then fell back and said, "Well, if the medical schools in Ohio won't join us to form a school of public health, then perhaps we can actually develop a consortium MPH program, fall back to one master's degree, and bring in the existing consortium partners for NEOUCOM, at least to start with. This would include The University of Akron, Kent State University, and Youngstown State University.

Interviewer: *Was there enough loss of support at this point where your idea was going down?*

Bill Keck: For the school of public health? Yes. It was going down. I was pretty sure that it was dead. We went from seven to four partners, and then another one dropped out.

Interviewer: *What kind of pressures did that place on you?*

You had been talking to people, they were coming to meetings, and you were doing your planning. What does it do to you when you're the person putting this thing together and people are popping out?

Bill Keck: It's a disappointment.

Interviewer: *Is it worse when no one comes to a party?*

Bill Keck: Yes, because there had been so much work put into it. But it was clear that it just wasn't going to work the way we'd initially thought about it. So we said, "Well, we've put a lot of the work in to this already, can we salvage it somehow? Can we find other partners for a sort of reduced vision of what we can do?"

NEOUCOM was an unusual medical school offering a combined BS/MD degree built on a consortium of the three universities I just mentioned. Each of those universities would admit one third of the medical student class out of high school for two years of pre-med studies, and then the class would come together for four years of medical school. These institutions already had a strong history of working together and when approached were eager to form a consortium Master of Public Health program. Cleveland State University was also quite interested in this idea and quickly joined us, giving us a five institution collaborative MPH program in northeast Ohio. A number of years later we added a sixth partner when Ohio University in southeast Ohio petitioned to join us.

In the end, the Toledo folks went ahead and developed their three institutional consortium MPH program, and Ohio State developed its school of public health. From our perspective, instead of trying to coordinate across the state, we were coordinating around here. As it all came together for us, I was able to get Dr. Amy Lee involved in its development and soon hired her to run it.

Interviewer: When you were talking with the entity that said that they were moving forward to plan their own school of public health but still wanted to plan with you, you said, "No, it's not in your interest." Why did you make that decision?

Bill Keck: Because I didn't think it was in their interest.

Interviewer: Has it been your experience that people who say to you openly, "We're not sure we are going to do this," in fact don't?

Bill Keck: Yes.

Interviewer: So by the time you verbalized it, you knew their track was already set to move in another direction.

Bill Keck: Something needed to have changed dramatically somewhere else to reorient them, and that wasn't likely to happen.

These were colleagues—even friends to some degree. It was important to be as straight with them as I could. I didn't want to waste their time and end up at the same place later.

Interviewer: One of the interesting things is that even though the grouping that came together wasn't the way you initially envisioned it, it exponentially increased the number of programs in the state, to the point where, really, if it had been that way when you started, you probably never would have pursued the consortium at all. Ohio State had their program; Toledo had theirs.

Bill Keck: And now, actually, Cincinnati has its own, Cleveland has its own, Toledo has its own, Dayton has its own, Athens has its own, Berea has its own, we have our own, and now we have two schools of public health because Ohio State developed its school, and then Kent State dropped out of our consortium to form their own school.

So now Amy's MPH program [The Consortium of Eastern Ohio Master of Public Health Program; CEOMPH] went from six partners to five. It does appear that the major constant is change.

Interviewer: You hit a home run, but it's really hard to have consortium members leave again and again. And yet, if you look at what was accomplished globally, if you put aside the fact they came in and then left, what they got from the program was the vision. They had the strength to do it on their own, but they didn't have the vision. They took your vision, and they ran with it. But if you look at what was accomplished, and you put aside what happened to the consortium, society's goal was met, even though your original goal wasn't met.

So you have to be careful with collaboration because you might define an outcome as a failure personally, yet it was a wonderful success.

Bill Keck: We have nine public health training programs in a state that had almost none.

Interviewer: *What advice do you have for people to live with that reality?*

Bill Keck: You have to be reasonably flexible in all of this. You have to understand that the more complex the relationships are, the more difficult they are to develop and maintain. That complexity increases the likelihood that something is going to go wrong somewhere along the way.

So you focus on the vision. What do we want to accomplish? We want to have a career track and public health training. We want to not only have a career track for current students but we also want people working in the discipline to be able to go back and get a degree while they're working—at a reasonable price. So we want to improve the capacity and the performance of public health. The end result we were looking for isn't the consortium; it is expanded opportunities to train the public health workforce, improve the quality of public health practice, and, hopefully, eventually improve public health status.

We're just arguing about which way to get there, so if you've got that goal in mind and one road is blocked, you look for another road.

Interviewer: *There were people who were in your position who had a vision—an unusual vision—and they went through something like you went through. They were mad at every single entity that walked away, especially when they took the ideas and ran with it on their own.*

Why didn't you get angry? How could you navigate what had to be personal disappointment? Here you had a vision you'd worked on for years, you'd attended meetings, and made phone calls, and put in maybe 1,000 hours for something that you personally didn't have any benefit from at all. It wasn't like there was any additional income involved for your work; it was strictly a public service thing. It wasn't even in your job description.

Bill Keck: I considered it part of my job description because I was hired to link academia and public health.

Interviewer: *That's a stretch, to think you had to create a consortium.*

Bill Keck: But a lot of things happened in the interim after I came to town, so I did what I could to take advantage of opportunities that arose, and developing these academic connections was one. And then getting the academic partners to focus on public health practice was another. That's not a small issue.

NARRATIVE #5

ON THE UNLIKELY CREATION OF A FEDERALLY QUALIFIED HEALTH CENTER (FQHC) WHICH BEGAN WITH THE VISION OF ONE DETERMINED STUDENT

Bill Keck: Into the 1990's there was no FQHC in Akron, which meant that Akron did not have a publicly funded source of primary care for people with no access to health insurance, either government-provided insurance or private insurance. There was no lower-cost option, if you will, and we had a significant area of town that was poorly served medically.

FQHCs are community-based organizations developed in medically underserved areas that provide comprehensive primary care and preventive care, including health, oral, and mental health/substance abuse services to people of all ages, regardless of their ability to pay or health insurance status. FQHCs operate under a consumer board of directors governance structure and function under the supervision of the Health Resources and Services Administration (HRSA), which is part of the United States Department of Health and Human Services (HHS).

I had explored this several times after I became health director in 1976, but there wasn't money for new FQHC's at that point, so I was discouraged from applying by the federal agency involved in this since they said, "We don't have the resources, no matter how good your application is. We just can't open any new ones at this point."

Several years after that, a young black male student going to Cleveland State University came to the health department and found his way to my office saying he would like to look at data for a school project. He was interested in any data we had that related to access to service and levels of health in the community. We were quite used to getting these sorts of requests. I had brought students in myself many times, so we said, "Sure."

We provided a lot of information for him and sent him off to others for more.

It turns out he was particularly interested in Akron because even though he was from Cleveland, he had relatives here and had learned from his relatives that their major source for health services was emergency rooms, which of course, was quite expensive and a poor way to provide primary care.

So he was interested in seeing what could be done to change that. I gave him a lot of credit; he was assertive and calm in his approach.

The next thing I knew, he actually showed up saying he had gotten an area of Akron declared a medically underserved area by the Department of Health and Human Services [DHHS]—a prerequisite for the establishment of an FQHC— put an application together for a FQHC, and sent it in. He had done all of this without any interaction with us other than our providing some data for him.

He had also put together a board of directors for his center in order to meet the requirements of an application. As chair, he had secured a union and civil rights activist from Akron, and had brought in a number of people from Cleveland as members of the board.

Their application was turned down by the federal government. They were told, "It's a nice start, but you have a lot more work to do. You need to get more involvement with local health service providers like hospitals and health departments."

They came to me at that point and asked me to get involved with them. I did not relish working with the chairman of the board who had been chosen; he was a difficult personality. When I looked at the board members from Cleveland and did some investigation there, I became uneasy about some of them, first figuring that they should be from the area to be served in Akron, and second, as I looked more into their backgrounds I wasn't sure they were appropriate for an FQHC board. In addition, the idea was that the Cleveland student would become the executive director of this new organization, so he was essentially creating an organization that he wanted to run with a board of his choosing.

So I hesitated, but after a lot of thought and discussion with my deputy director, Greg Ervin, my administrative assistant, Sue Phillips, and my wife, Ardith, I decided that it was appropriate for the health director (me) to try to make this happen. Akron could benefit from it, so I agreed to work with them. My formal role at that time was as a consultant.

As we began to work together I told them that in order to get federal approval, we would have to revamp the board to make it Akron-based and represent the population served. I couldn't say that the local person couldn't be the chair. He was very interested in the position and qualified, even though he was sometimes difficult to work with.

The biggest question, however, was how would it be funded? Where would the local support required to match federal funds come from? I knew they didn't get their grant approved at first because they didn't answer that question and didn't have any involvement with local healthcare providers.

I also knew that most FQHCs funded in other parts of the country or the state had started out as something else that had evolved into a FQHC. In other words, they had a building, employees, and services being provided, and just changed the structure and governance to meet FQHC requirements, usually while expanding services.

We didn't have any of that. We were starting from scratch, which was very unusual.

I also knew that at that time we had two adult hospital systems and a children's hospital, and unless the hospitals were involved and supportive, the project wouldn't have a chance. And while the hospitals were competitive, the health department was often in a position to get them to collaborate on issues related to community health.

So I went to the chief executive officers of the three hospital systems, discussed this, and they agreed that it made sense. After several meetings with them they made it clear that they would be involved and provide some financial support. They agreed the health department should spearhead it because that would help them to be collaborative. If one of them was the primary organizer, then the other hospitals would perhaps have some pause. We put together a hospital/health department advisory group and tried to work with the existing board of trustees and its chairman.

With the hospital promise of involvement and a revamped organizational structure, but the continued involvement of some folks on the board that had concerned me, they sent a second application in to the Bureau of Primary Care in DHHS for review without consulting me. The application named the same person as executive director, the same board chair, and many of the same board members that had been included in the first application. It looked like it was going to be approved, but between the time it was sent in and the evaluation of the application was completed, I felt I needed to intervene. I believed the proposed executive director [the student] was not qualified for that position, and I didn't trust some on the board. There was a racial overtone to this as well, because we had a black man coming up as executive director, and we had people in the approving body who were very anxious to see more black people in positions of importance. All that was appropriate; I just didn't think these folks were qualified to do the jobs required.

The hospitals also were uncertain, and as I had discussions with them, it turns out if it was going to go ahead as it was, I couldn't guarantee their continued support and involvement. So I actually called our congressman at the time, explained the situation, and said he should be sure that the approving body asks a series of questions I gave him about the application.

He did that, and the approval process stopped. The federal project director used that as an opportunity to talk to the chair of the board and the student soon to be executive director [he hoped] about the necessity of changing a few things.

The short version is that eventually the two of them agreed to revisit the application. They really had no choice, but the chair of the board was gracious enough to step back. Actually, he came and asked me to be chair of the board and said he would resign as chair. He understood that it would take somebody else to bring the board together and get the new organization moving. He said, "My role is getting it started. I've gotten it started, but I have no experience running things. I need somebody who can do that." I think that's exactly what the federal project director had told him.

So after that happened, things clarified. The federal grant was approved, we reconstituted the board of which I was now chair, and we went ahead with the student—ex-student now—as interim executive director while we began a search for a qualified executive director. We were soon able to hire a well-qualified black woman. This helped us with the race issue, and we kept the student on as deputy executive director to give him time to develop his skills under a strong mentor.

Once we got the grant approved and the FQHC started, the former chairman of the board became very friendly and quite supportive in the community.

Interviewer: *This is a tough story because you have a kid, a young person who came up with an idea.*

Bill Keck: Yes, very tough.

Interviewer: *I get the impression that you kept a cordial relationship with both the chair of the board who needed to be replaced and the student who needed more experience to become executive director? How do you keep a good relationship with people when you're letting them go?*

Bill Keck: Keeping a cordial relationship with the former board chairman was easy. I believe he was relieved to pass the baton to someone else because he didn't have the experience required to develop a new board, develop working relationships with health care providers, and hire staff. It was not so easy with the student. He was not happy. I think he understood from the funders that he needed to be replaced, and the hospitals made it clear that they would pull out if he wasn't, so the hospitals had my back in this all the way along. Also, the student was able to focus on his primary goal of getting an FQHC established. To make that happen, he would have to delay his personal goal of being its director.

There were times during the early development of this project when these people threatened me. They threatened to go public and "expose" us—the hospitals and me—as being uncooperative. I actually went to a meeting with the three hospital execs, and I sat down with them and said, "You know, it may be time to just cut this loose with all this subterfuge going on. If they are going to go public and accuse us of something, then it's not good for our reputations or our institutions'."

They looked at me and said, "No, we're not going to quit. We have your back; you have the full resources of the three hospitals at your back. We will go ahead." It was amazing.

So we persevered, and we were able to work things out over time.

Interviewer: *What is the lesson here?*

Bill Keck: I guess it is try to understand the personalities and the issues involved. Look for ways to resolve conflict that end up being as positive as possible for all the participants.

Interviewer: How do people respond when you tell them in a meeting that things aren't going well?

Bill Keck: Well, in the particular meeting I'm thinking about, I wasn't sure the people I was working with and the organizational structure they were proposing would really allow the project to be successful—certainly, not to thrive.

And because the folks I was working with had this adversarial mentality, "If you're not with me, your agin' me," they threatened to put out public stories saying we wouldn't collaborate with them.

I said, "I don't need this, and certainly the hospitals don't need this." They were already considered non-collaborative in the community, so I didn't want another story like this coming out.

I went to the three hospital administrators at the time, sat down, told them what I was facing, and said, "At this point, I'm wondering whether we should continue, because we don't need all this bad publicity. We don't need a public fight over this, and if that's the way this is going to go, then we're just going to have trouble all along. I'm not sure the juice is worth the squeeze."

So I just said, "Right now, my recommendation is that we pull out."

They said, "We're going to move ahead; stick in there. We have your back; don't worry about us."

Interviewer: The tough part about this is what I'll call the "iffy" nature of these situations. It's one thing to sit here today and talk about it, but at the moment, this was not fun. And you thought it was bad enough that you were ready to get off the horse.

Bill Keck: Yes, after being very publicly on the horse. Ardith and I had lots of discussions about that here at home.

Interviewer: *A lot of this doesn't feel comfortable. Our readers need to understand that. They're going to feel threatened, insulted, unimportant, and disrespected. They may feel "whatever."*

It is not an easy space to live in when you've got a serious problem with a collaboration, and you have to go the people you report to and share it with them.

Some aspects of collaboration are emotionally tough, and this is one of them. Do you have any advice for someone going through this for the first time? How do you survive that?

Bill Keck: I think one thing to do is ask yourself, "What would have happened if my worst fears had come true and I hadn't been upfront about it?" Suppose I hadn't said anything to the hospital folks, and the next thing I know I've got some reporter calling me because so-and-so is complaining publicly that we're shooting this down; we're not collaborative; we're not players; we have our own agenda; we're not making enough money—whatever it is.

It's much better to be upfront with that, understand it, and confront it.

Interviewer: *What is the problem strategically when you've got a situation where people you've been reporting to have been surprised, as in this scenario you said was possible?*

Bill Keck: You're defensive, and it looks like you're not managing it well, that perhaps you weren't aware of problems that were developing.

Interviewer: *So the downside is that you could be perceived as an incompetent manager.*

Bill Keck: Yes, and your reputation could suffer.

Interviewer: *You could also be perceived as someone who withheld problems from them. Of course, the hospitals saying what they did had a positive result; it meant you could deal with things the way you wanted to deal with them.*

On the other hand, it's also true that the very reason people go to the press is to embarrass someone, so it had a serious potential downside. All the more reason to share what could be going wrong with those you report to.

Do you have any other advice regarding controlling your emotions and not saying what you think in front of those who oppose you? How do you get your canoe through the rocks without putting a hole in the birch bark?

Bill Keck: Well, of course, this wasn't a surprise to me. I knew that there were these issues all the way along, and I was trying to manage them. However, I was getting to the point where I thought I was not going to be able to manage this anymore, or I couldn't predict well enough what was going to happen.

Interviewer: *You had gotten to the point where you were going to jump out of the plane with a parachute and get out, but you didn't jump.*

Bill Keck: That would be a hit to my ego and reputation, of course, if we pulled out. But that's life.

Interviewer: *But you were working with people who didn't have much experience. Do you have any other advice for people who are going to have to navigate similar waters?*

Bill Keck: Don't wait too long to say there's a problem. If you have a good working relationship with the folks you report to or backers, then don't surprise them. Let them know when you can that there may be some problems developing here.

I had done that too. So they had time to think about it. But then I came to them and said, "You know, I'm really concerned about these latest developments."

Interviewer: *Well, they threatened to go to the press; all of a sudden, they upped the ante. They started to point their cannons at you, and you said, "I don't want to have cannons pointed at me."*

Ardith Keck: I think it's crucial to always be honest and always keep everybody informed along the way. That's one of Bill's strengths. He's willing to do that regardless of what it means, because sometimes it doesn't mean good things.

Interviewer: *Sometimes people will take weakness and use it against you. If you're in a strategic situation which is "iffy," those who want to damage it might. So there are some risks.*

What can we learn from this story about the young student with big ideas for public service through a FQHC? [Federally Qualified Health Center]

Ardith Keck: Bill and I talked about this at some length, and he felt that it was his job to do this—not "Above and Beyond" at all, but his job.

Bill Keck: Well, that's true. As director of health, I was responsible for trying to improve health status, and included in that was getting services to people who didn't have access to them otherwise. This was a chance to get affordable primary care to a lot of people who had no access to it.

There clearly was some risk in this, but there was also potential gain.

Interviewer: *What were the risks?*

Bill Keck: The risk that it wouldn't work, that it would fail somehow. Some of the consequences of that kind of failure would be an issue for me in my job and reputation in the community.

You don't want to take on something like that and not have it work out.

Interviewer: What do you think the chances were of this project not working out?

Bill Keck: I don't know how to quantify that. Certainly the risk was real because these characters were involved, and they were politically motivated in some ways that could make life uncomfortable for me if they wished to. So there was definitely some risk.

There was a lot of risk besides just that, quite frankly, because the federal government, The Department of Health and Human Services, had never funded a FQHC before that didn't have something already in existence.

They'd never funded one that was a partnership between a health department and a group of hospitals. They were somewhat leery about hospital involvement because in their experience, hospitals tended to focus on their bottom line and not so much on making services available, so the feds were taking some risks in this too. To the credit of our local hospitals, however, they pushed us hard to be successful and really helped us in many ways to meet the basic requirements of a FQHC.

I also had excellent support back at the health department. Sue Phillips, who served as my administrative assistant in that time, kept things organized. She was very smart, very intuitive, and very supportive. She kept my life moving. Gregory Ervin, the deputy director of health in Akron, and I made a good management team. Both of them understood and supported the work I was doing at the medical school, the health department, and professional organizations at the state and national level. They provided me with excellent counsel and took on as many of the tasks involved as they could.

Interviewer: I did not know that this type of arrangement was new for the nation. I assumed others had done it before.

Bill Keck: Apparently not.

Interviewer: That's interesting because it's not only out-of-the-box here; it's out of the box for the whole country. So it was a much bigger step into the unknown.

What goes through your mind when you come across people who put selfish concerns over service of mankind?

Bill Keck: I'm a bit regretful about it, I guess. It's a shame that another opportunity is lost.

Interviewer: What do you lose if you're selfish? If you are that person who won't go help somebody else, who won't go above and beyond, who won't give a young student a chance, what do you lose? You lose something.

Bill Keck: Yes, you do. You lose opportunity, as I said, if part of your job or reason for being there is to take advantage of those opportunities to serve. Those are things that the community or the people you are supposed to serve don't get that they could have, or might have, if you'd tried harder.

Interviewer: Are you saying you have to bear the responsibility that you didn't help when you could have?

Bill Keck: Yes, I think that's right.

Interviewer: Isn't that a heavy load for a person to carry?

Bill Keck: The fact that they didn't take advantage of the opportunities? Most of them, I suspect, feel maybe they just don't want to put the work in or take the risk.

Interviewer: They're expressing an entitlement attitude: "I'm doing my job. I don't want to do any more work, I won't get paid any more, and Lord knows I'm not appreciated anyway in this job. It's far more work than I'm getting paid for already." I think that maybe what you lose is your humanity. That's what it costs you when you do not help your fellow man. You can lose your humanity, or you can add to it. It's dynamic. You can become more sensitive and more caring, which comes with more respect. Most people don't say, "I respect that individual. They didn't do anything for anyone."

Bill Keck: That's right.

Interviewer: How do you learn to think out of the box and act on it?

Bill Keck: There may be times that you would honestly decide, "I just can't make it work."

Interviewer: Ardith, what themes are we hitting on here that resonate with you?

Bill does things other people wouldn't do. I'm guessing that 80% of the people would not have moved forward with this because of the tremendous amount of time involved—not with that mix of involved people. Most had no experience in the field. That's risk.

It wasn't that they were bad people; they just couldn't get it done on their own.

Reality would say, "Wrong team, wrong guys, not enough experience, just a student. Too much work for me. My own solution already got turned down. If I'm going to go back in, I'm going to go back in with my own solution—done my way."

Bill didn't do that.

Ardith Keck: What Bill isn't saying, because he wouldn't, is that it was because of the respect other people have for him that he got this done, and there are probably far fewer people who could do it simply because it took that kind of respect.

Interviewer: True, but he doesn't think in those terms—he does not think about the respect that is his at all. In his thinking, it was done for other reasons. But you're saying the fact is he got it done because they respected him, because when he said something, they listened.

Ardith Keck: Most people would not have been able to do it.

Interviewer: It was going to be hard and challenging. Bill, why did you work with them?

Bill Keck: Because I wanted to see the FQHC in place. I thought it would make a big difference for a lot of folks, that the community had the need for it, could justify that need, and should be among those communities funded to provide those services.

Interviewer: You had already mentally determined the concept was valid and you knew it was the right thing to do.

Bill Keck: I believed it was the right thing to do.

Interviewer: Why were you willing to work with the wrong team, if I may be so blunt?

Bill Keck: They'd already done a lot of the work! They had been rejected largely because they hadn't really connected well with this community, but the basic description of what they wanted to do—the basic analysis—was all done.

Interviewer: Do you think that was valid?

Bill Keck: Yes.

Interviewer: Did you think the people they submitted it to thought it was valid?

Bill Keck: Yes, because they told them, "That's a good start."

Interviewer: Did they have to be black to tell that story?

Bill Keck: No, but it helped.

Interviewer: How come they were able to tell that story and the Feds listened? After all, you'd done the same sometime earlier and the Feds hadn't listened. Was it because they represented the minority and the impoverished?

Bill Keck: I suspect that's part of it. I don't really know. I wasn't on the receiving end. I didn't know much about what was going on until they actually got the rejection letter, and then they shared with me how far they'd gone. That was a surprise to me. See, he'd come in asking for information and data and so on, which we gave him. And then after several sessions like that, the next thing I heard was, "Gee, we submitted this, and it wasn't accepted." The shortcomings were this community connection with hospitals and other organizations and institutions in the city. The rest of it was pretty good.

NARRATIVE #6

ABOVE AND BEYOND

Interviewer: Talk to me about "Above and Beyond."

Bill Keck: It's hard for me because I didn't see my work as being "Above and Beyond."

Interviewer: In general, then, why is reaching for excellence more than other people do a good thing?

Bill Keck: Well, it's looking for outcomes—looking for results that may be difficult to come by without being willing to spend extra time. As you've suggested before, in any managerial position like mine you have the daily humdrum of administration, finance, program development and evaluation, reporting, and making decisions about what comes next.

Some of that is fairly easy to do because it exists within the construct of an existing organization that's set up to do these tasks. But seeing patients at clinics and inspecting restaurants—doing all the other things that a health department does—takes significant time and effort. I think I could have successfully stayed in the job just by making sure we had the people and resources to carry out that work well.

But clearly, part of the job was also assessing the health status of the community. We did that in some interesting ways, including hiring people with special skills to really do it well. When we looked at the results we could see where the problems were geographically and those problems could then be described in terms like socio-economic status, race, age, and gender.

It became clear that there were sections of the community of Akron that were much less healthy than others and were characterized by low socio-economic status, poor access to medical services, higher rates of both adult and infant mortality, and so on.

When you have that kind of information, you can't avoid asking, "What do you do to address your findings?" Much of what the health department did at that time was try to fill gaps in the healthcare system. That's why we had well-baby clinics, prenatal clinics, and immunization clinics. If everybody had access to good, preventively-oriented primary care, we wouldn't need any of those services in the health department.

In many ways, it was, in my view, a misuse of public health dollars to provide medical services when we should have been focusing even more on prevention of disease and injury and mitigating the social determinants of health. I was always struggling to find ways to have a greater impact on health status.

Interviewer: I *understand. So you're sharing with me how in your thinking, you weren't acting in the "above and beyond" mode. Your actions were a legitimate, appropriate extension of the charge that had been put in your care. You did impact the groups of people you wanted to touch with something they did need; therefore, it was part of your job description.*

Then why don't so many other people in the world do that?

Bill Keck: [Laughs]

Interviewer: Maybe *they didn't read their job description?*

Bill Keck: Maybe that's it. I don't know! It's sort of been a pattern for me. I did it in Kentucky, and I did it here.

Interviewer: Why?

Bill Keck: I see these things that need to be done, and if I'm in a position to get them done, then I assess whether I have the skill and the time to do it. If I think I do, I go ahead.

And it worked out pretty well.

Interviewer: *There's a theme of interest here. This entire story could be called, "Above and Beyond."*

Bill Keck: I wouldn't have had to do it, that's true.

Interviewer: *You performed more service than what was required; it was public service. Is that part of being in collaborations—the idea that you go above and beyond what is necessary to serve?*

This idea of "Above and Beyond." has not been talked about in any of the book interviews!

Bill Keck: Well, it's hard to define what that is, isn't it? Because it comes back to the mission, right? If the idea is to impact the community's health in a positive way, then you look at a variety of ways to do that.

Interviewer: *So my point is what is the role of "Above and Beyond" in this whole picture?*

Ardith is shaking her head, saying, "Yeah."

Ardith Keck: That's part of Bill's success—that capability.

Interviewer: *[To Ardith] What is the phrase you'd use? I've used "Above and Beyond."*

Ardith Keck: "Above and Beyond" is a great description of it.

Interviewer: So he had no qualms about adding on 3,000 hours of work for which he wouldn't be paid a dime more, and was never asked to do, and was really out-of-the-box.

Ardith Keck: Exactly.

Interviewer: And yet for him that was considered standard operating procedure, and Ardith, you're saying that was part of his success. Why?

Ardith Keck: Because he doesn't look at a job as just a certain number of hours. He thinks, "How do I get this done? How do I get success?"

Interviewer: It's a total service-centered attitude on a deep level. Bill, is this book a tutorial on going "Above and Beyond," and we're going to ask people to consider doing what you did, which was to tack on 3,000 hours?

Bill Keck: 3,000 hours isn't really accurate. Who knows what it is?

Interviewer: Well, it's a lot. I'll bet it was close to 3,000 hours. Why should someone be willing to go beyond what's asked to be done?

Ardith Keck: It's just a higher vision. If you have a higher vision, and you want to accomplish that vision, you'll do whatever it takes.

Bill Keck: I don't know how to answer that.

Interviewer: Sadly, most people are selfish.

Bill Keck: I know.

Interviewer: And they have a limited number of hours. I know that in music, for example, you may ask the question, "Why continue to work?" In an article I recently wrote, I said, "This is what you need to do to study the music.

Listen to 20 versions, look at the chord progressions and decide how the melody fits into the chord progressions, play the piece 50 times, decide stylistically how you want to play it, record it, play it for friends, get input, and on and on." I looked at the list and said, "Now I don't know if somebody is really going to want to do that, because you could play the piece way back here on the list." But the answer is if you want artistic excellence, better than anyone else can play something, you have to do that work because excellence does not come easily.

And learning the piece, memorizing it, and playing it are just really the beginning of developing the artistry. I think that there's a concept here that's very similar. As you reach towards an ideal, you become more ideal.

Bill Keck: Maybe.

Ardith Keck: It's a little bit like competing in the Olympics; it's a little bit like working on any craft. If you believe in success, then you do what it takes.

Interviewer: *People look to you as being more capable, people buy into it, and respect it. You know you've done the best you can do, and you can grow as a human being through your service to others.*

A lot of things in public health make no sense at all on any basis other than helping people. It's not a field you're going to make a lot of money in: you're not going to retire as a multimillionaire.

This idea of "Above and Beyond," which your lives reflect, is an important idea for people all around the world to be exposed to and learn from.

And it may explain 50% of why you've both been so successful.

Time and again, people saw that Bill is cool and calm, he has a vision, and he won't quit. They thought, "We'll be surprised where this thing's going to go and what he can do."

Interviewer's comments: While the idea of going "above and beyond" is not the way Dr. Keck looks at his life and work, he did, in fact, go above and beyond many times in his career.

There are many components to this dynamic, all of them reflective of fine character:

- Demonstrating a high level of collaborative skills
- Keeping a goal in mind for many years
- Skillfully taking a big risk for a big reward
- Showing zero fear of additional work
- Exhibiting patience
- Putting others above self
- Giving credit to others
- Looking closely at what you're really trying to achieve

The above are all an integral part of why Dr. Keck developed a reputation as a man who can get things done that others can't with superb results.

REFLECTIONS ON THE LEADERSHIP STYLE OF BILL KECK

This section of the book consists of interviews of three people who worked closely with Bill Keck. They are included to illustrate the value of cultivating the respect and support of key staff members (Gregory Ervin and Sue Phillips) who were in a position to greatly facilitate the activities of their "boss," and to demonstrate the value of having a true champion for a collaborative cause in organizations that are part of a collaborative venture (Walter Evans—not his real name in this interview).

GREGORY ERVIN

Gregory Ervin served as the deputy director of health for the Akron City Health Department from May 1986 to March 2002 and as the Jackson County Health Commissioner in southeastern Ohio from June 2002 to July 2013. Prior to working with Dr. Keck in Akron, he worked for the Ohio Department of Health for 14 years in various administrative positions. Ervin earned his master of public health degree at the University of Tennessee in 1976. He has retired and currently works as a consultant for the Area Agency on Aging, District 7 in southern Ohio promoting wellness programs.

Interviewer: *Do you have some observations about the experience of creating the Federally Qualified Health Center (FQHC) with Dr. Bill Keck that can help us understand what happened from your perspective? What do these observations say about Dr. Keck's collaborative style?*

Gregory Ervin: As I recall, Bill Keck was very much involved with the community and trying to improve the health status of everyone in the Greater Akron area. I retired from the Akron Health Department in the spring of 2002 and took a couple of months off before becoming the health commissioner for Jackson County, a rural county in southeastern Ohio. I grew up there, and the only reason I left the Akron Health Department was to go back home and become a health commissioner on my own.

In Akron we always talked about the Three C's: the highway that connected Cincinnati, Columbus, and Cleveland, the Three C Highway. At the Akron Health Department we thought of the Three C's as cooperation, coordination, and collaboration as we interacted with our community partners.

I found in Akron that the community played well together, much more so than in many other communities. I believe Dr. Keck's leadership style helped build this sense of community and collaboration. I found the same to be true in rural southeastern Ohio. We found ways to work together because the resources were so scarce. We had to cooperate, coordinate, and collaborate with our community partners in order get things done. Probably just as important as the Three C's was communication. You always talked with your partners, and they knew what you were doing. They knew you weren't trying to steal their programs because you thought you could do it better—or for any other reason.

A Cleveland State University student with the goal of improving access to primary care in Akron set up a meeting with Dr. Keck and started talking about setting up a FQHC in Akron. I believe his motivation was that his family in Cleveland had access to FQHC services, and they received high quality health service through them. When he came to the Akron area, he discovered that there was no FQHC. Many families in the minority community didn't have access to health services. At the time Akron was the only major metropolitan area in Ohio without a FQHC.

The student had the idea and the concept. He also had the fire in the belly to see a project through. He was really willing to work hard to achieve his goal of establishing an FQHC in Akron. What he didn't know, he made up for in perseverance, and he kept working at it. So he was an available resource, and certainly Dr. Keck believed that working with him made a lot of sense because he could do things, particularly in the minority community to engage individuals and get some excitement there, which would be more difficult for us to do from the downtown Akron public health agency.

It was kind of a gamble, but there wasn't that much to lose because we didn't have that type of community health center in Akron.

Dr. Keck was the health director for the city of Akron, and I was the deputy director—kind of an inside manager. At that time we had over 200 employees. Bill was very active and engaged in the community. He was involved with NEOUCOM—Northeastern Ohio Universities College of Medicine—now Northeast Ohio Medical University. The medical school was part of his job responsibilities and provided an academic connection for public health, like a teaching health department. Bill was out making community contacts, building and maintaining community relationships, and I was kind of responsible for making sure all the bills were paid, the staff was paid, the grants were submitted, and the department complied with all of the city requirements for personnel and finances. I went to all the City Council meetings and was the primary contact with the city of Akron. Together, we really worked to maintain positive relationships with the other city departments and Akron's elected officials.

There's a separation in public health from the city, yet we were a city department. So we tried to act, look, and sound just like every other city department 99 times out of 100. However, we could step away because we were governed by a separate board of health, the health commission. The health department still relied on the city for much of its funding through the city's general fund, so maintaining a positive relationship with the city and its elected officials was very important.

What I think most about Dr. Keck is his building relationships and working with everyone in the community. He set the stage for the eventual combination of all three health departments in Summit County: the Akron Health Department, the Barberton Health Department, and the Summit County Health Department. Dr. Keck worked very closely with the other two health directors. They considered the entire county as their service area or patient. We worked closely together, and the three health departments shared grants and resources. This collaboration, cooperation, and coordination helped set the stage so that when funding significantly declined and in some cases eventually disappeared, the Summit County Health Department was able to absorb the Akron and Barberton Health Departments.

I don't think the eventual consolidation of the three health departments would have been possible without Dr. Keck's work to build those relationships with the other public health agencies and all the political figures it takes to forge a countywide public health agency. The consolidations occurred probably five or six years after Dr. Keck retired; his collaborative management style helped prepare the environment for the combined operation.

Building the relationships with the student from Cleveland and the person chosen by the student to chair the board of directors of the developing FQHC were certainly important.

The board chair was a social studies professor at The University of Akron and a strong advocate for the minority community. He was somewhat of a firebrand, and many community leaders were reluctant to become involved with him. Both the student and the board chair were individuals somewhat outside the normal circle of public health officials. They had a different skill set than we were accustomed to dealing with at the local and state level. However, they each had unique abilities and certainly an interest in improving healthcare for the residents of Akron. Dr. Keck recognized their skills, abilities, and passion and worked with them to establish the Akron Community Health Resources FQHC. Dr. Keck believed it was much better to invite a critical community activist into the tent [the problem resolution process] than to keep them on the outside. Once invited into the tent, the one-time critic is more likely to work to help resolve the issue at hand. If the critic remains outside the tent, they are most likely to remain critical of any solution made without their input.

Interviewer: Based on your years of experience and the number of times you dealt with people in positions of leadership in public health, did you observe that people's collaboration skills varied?

Gregory Ervin: Well, sure. Everyone has strengths, and certainly we all have some weaknesses. Some displayed much better leadership and understanding of where their peers were coming from in a particular area. They could look at the big picture and see that they were all trying to provide services to a given community.

Some people are better at going into a group and engaging them in the process. Certainly it works better when you're not pretending or not acting as the expert—that you know all the answers when you engage the community in the process— get their input, and eventually help lead them to conclude that a particular action is going to be beneficial for their health and the health of their community.

Some of us are better at getting the buy-in; other people's approach is, "I've got the MPH or the Doctorate in Public Health; I know what's best." That may be the case, but you need to get that input from all those other individuals so that they can come to the same conclusion.

Consensus building is certainly more of an art than a science. You need to understand others' points of view if you expect to build consensus. It requires a unique style of leadership. Certainly, Dr. Keck had the ability to do that; he certainly had the perseverance. He might not get 10 yards on the first play, but if he got three yards, then three more yards, and then three more yards, he could accomplish a complex community project. Dr. Keck was willing to work to make the incremental improvements and take the many steps needed to accomplish a task.

Interviewer: As you look at Bill's career in public health, what should we find inspiration from? What is the good pattern we can learn from?

Gregory Ervin: I was working for the Ohio Department of Health (ODH) when the opportunity to compete for deputy director with the Akron Health Department came up. At ODH I was in administration and the top civil service person that had to deal with all the newly appointed deputy directors that were coming in in the mid 80s. The Ohio Department of Health was becoming more and more political. I enjoyed working in administration at ODH, but when the opportunity came up to compete for the position in Akron as the deputy director and work with Dr. Keck, I had no hesitation to leave ODH and relocate from Columbus to Akron. I knew enough about Dr. Keck's management style that it would be a great learning opportunity for me to work with him.

I was really pleased to have that chance because I had worked with Dr. Keck when I was with ODH. Dr. Keck was on several state committees, and I processed his travel expenses. I got to know him a little bit and had opportunities to talk with him.

I knew enough about what Dr. Keck was doing in Akron and that he was someone that I'd like to work for at some point in time. His ability to work with a very diverse staff and build a program that could serve all of the community interested me, and I wanted to learn from him how to be a better health professional.

In the mid 80s, Management by Objectives and Results [MBO/R] was one of the more popular management tools used to help increase productivity. We met with all the Akron Health Department managers quarterly. They had to develop their goals, objectives, and the methods they would use to enhance their programs and services to the community. To help achieve their objectives, we reviewed them and had continuous input from the managers. He kept his managers focused and engaged in the MBO/R process and the results.

Dr. Keck was very good at keeping folks on task and helping them see the big picture so that the nursing director and the nutrition director were not just focused on their particular programs; they could see nutrition impacted nursing—the component that nutrition could provide to health education. The general health educators could pick up certain things from the nutrition director that they could apply in health education.

Dr. Keck was extremely apt at maximizing individuals' skills, and he understood that we do some things better than others, He could find the right place to put a person so that they could do the best job for the agency.

One of the small mementos he had on his desk was the Velvet Hammer Award that he received from nurse supervisors at the health department. I think that pretty much typifies him—a velvet hammer. He could keep pounding away at it, yet the impacts were not such that they would knock out the other person.

Dr. Keck was never overly impressed by his own credentials. I think that's important. I've worked with a lot of folks that were more impressed by their credentials than they should have been. They lost the common touch. Dr. Keck never lost that. As president of the American Public Health Association and in many other leadership positions, he was always a special, humble, caring individual, and I don't think I ever heard anyone speak ill of him.

"WALTER EVANS"

This is an interview with a professional who serves as a federal official in public health. Per his request, his name is not mentioned. We will call him "Walter Evans."

Interviewer: *It seemed unusual that Dr. Bill Keck was open to the idea of a Federally Qualified Health Center submitted by a student at Cleveland State University. And embracing it was different from what others would have done. What does this say about Bill, and what does it say about seeing beyond our own selfish concerns in service to the public in public health?*

Walter Evans: There are a few lessons. One is Bill is a good judge of character and capabilities, so he was able to assess that this individual had skills that could help move this project forward.

The second is he had a strong desire to see additional service delivery capacity built in Akron, and he wisely utilized someone who had an ability to move that project forward, recognizing that the individual might not be the one to carry it to full completion but would be well suited to do much of the legwork to get the project off the ground.

If this individual hadn't been there, it probably wouldn't have taken off.

Interviewer: *As you look back on your career, have you seen instances where people were not able to put their ego aside and good ideas died because they wouldn't work with somebody?*

Walter Evans: It takes a big thinker and a person with an open mind to see possibilities within a person when they're not obvious to everyone, and Bill has the ability to look and listen. He is really open to an idea and interested in making something happen without having to own every piece of the project. Bill clearly bestowed trust in people to accomplish what they committed to doing, and then he supported them in moving towards those goals.

Interviewer: *Why else do you think Bill was so successful in his career and is so successful now with his work with Cuba. What's unique about Dr. Bill Keck?*

Walter Evans: There are a number of things that are unique about Bill. He strives hard to see the big picture. I think he has the average person's interests at heart, so when he's trying to develop a health care system, he's thinking about the people who are supposed to be served, not about his own specific personal or professional interests.

He's not distracted by the incentives in the system that often move us away from getting people the services they need and toward other agendas.

Interviewer: *Is there anything else you'd like to add?*

Walter Evans: I'd add Bill's demeanor is one of kindness and affirmation.

I can't speak to how other people react to Bill, but he garnered my trust very quickly in the way he treated me and spoke to me. At the time, I was relatively new in my career in government service, and Bill was open and respectful, trying to understand what I could and couldn't do.

We didn't always agree. We actually had some pretty significant disagreements, but the difference between Bill and me, and so many other people, is that Bill actually listened. So when we disagreed, he took the time to hear my perspective and what was behind it.

Because we came together around mission and objectives, I believe we were able to overcome the challenges, and Bill was able to achieve the goal of building additional services for those in greatest need in Akron.

I'll tell you an interesting story.

I had spoken to the Cleveland State student who stepped forward to help bring the Akron FQHC idea together about him not having all the qualifications to be the program director. There was too much complexity involved.

However, when my boss met the student at a meeting in Chicago where the organizations interested in federal funding, or those that had already been funded, came together, my boss then changed directions and encouraged him to apply to be the director. That was a major mistake because the student wasn't ready to be a director. My boss was doing that for emotional reasons and because he didn't do his homework.

Major challenges ensued, and this affected Dr. Keck as well because he agreed the student wasn't ready to be the executive director. High-level management, however, wanted to reward the student for his great work and felt grooming him for the directorship was reasonable.

The board chair (a local NAACP representative) got involved on behalf of the student, so we had all sorts of communications going on. A variety of people from Akron were talking to other people in my organization that my staff were not working with, and it wasn't clear that I would remain the federal point person for the project.

It got to the point that the board chair realized the problems that were surfacing and asked the top leadership at my organization to make me the point person, but I wasn't at that meeting. And I was not feeling good about it. I was the one doing the work all along, and people who hadn't been involved who either didn't know the situation or had disregarded what they originally agreed to became part of the decision making process.

When the board chair walked out of that meeting, he apparently wanted me to be the point of contact, even though up to that point we had not agreed on all elements of the project. Fortunately, the top boss in my organization then asked me to continue as the point of contact and told everyone else that all communications would go through me from then on.

The board chair and Dr. Keck eventually camped out and met. There were some significant differences between those two in terms of their approaches, but we all agreed that we wanted the services for Akron, even if we disagreed over the individual who was to direct it. We wanted the same thing, and we needed to focus on that and move the project forward.

Dr. Keck and the NAACP gentleman started working well together because they were able to put their egos aside, focus on the end result, and become a powerful team.

The health center was eventually built

Interviewer: *This story helps to clarify how Bill functions. The challenge with him, of course, is that he won't say very much nice about himself even when I use my crowbar.*

Walter Evans: He's humble. Why have I stayed connected with Bill? Part of it is just respect. Secondly, he represents someone I thought could be helpful to me in my career at some point. I wanted to be connected with him because if things ever changed in Akron or in the State, I wanted someone like him in my orbit.

Bill presented things in a kind, respectful, but clear way, so I left that relationship in a very positive mode. He has a trail of people—like me—who have tremendous respect for him.

SUE PHILLIPS

Sue Phillips began her career with the Akron Health Department in March 1978. She was hired to work in the administration division, where she remained until her retirement in April 2010. Sue worked with the financial personnel of the health department until December 1980 when Dr. Keck's longtime assistant announced her retirement. Since there was a hiring freeze at the time, Dr. Keck and the deputy director had to choose someone from within the department to fill the position. Sue was selected and worked as Dr. Keck's assistant until his retirement in 2003.

Interviewer: *After learning that Dr. Bill Keck was open to working with a student who had the idea of a Federally Qualified Health Center, I thought that Bill's decision to support the effort was perhaps unique. I think most would have taken the idea and done it themselves with a more qualified team with experience in public health. This action on Bill's part was part of a pattern I call going "Above and Beyond." Do you have a comment as you worked with him during that time?*

Sue Phillips: I think he evidenced more heart and an attitude of serving others than one might typically expect from a health director. Dr. Keck was never shy about trying new things.

He was so good at being able to put the right people in the right places. If he took something on, he was going to see it through. I worked for him 25 of the 32 years that I worked for the city of Akron. When we had a new director come in upon Dr. Keck's retirement, the difference between Dr. Keck and the new director was so marked that I thought, "Gosh, how fortunate I was to work with an individual like Dr. Keck."

Interviewer: *How would you describe his method of working with people?*

Sue Phillips: Dr. Keck was so involved and so respected by his peers that he really put the Akron Health Department on the map. His involvement in the local community and on the state and national levels furthered the respect of the organization during his tenure.

He became so invested in everything he did. He had so much knowledge, and he was so good at putting people together and getting people to work with him. He's very humble, very kind, and never wanted to put too much on people.

Whenever he would get involved with some of the things that he did during his tenure as director of health, he would always come to me and say, "You know, if I go ahead with this, it's going to mean more work for you."

And I would say, "Yeah, that's cool," because I loved learning from him, and I was always willing to help him go forward. "If you think it's good, then I know it's good, and I'm on board."

Interviewer: Do you think he has personality characteristics that make him an ideal choice for collaborative effort?

Sue Phillips: Absolutely! No doubt in my mind. He just knows how to do it.

Interviewer: Do you remember the story about the Federally Qualified Health Center? What were your impressions of the chances of that being successful early on? Were you saying to yourself, "I just don't see how this is going to happen with this group?"

Bill had a chairman of the board that was the wrong guy; he had an executive director that had been forced on him that was the wrong guy. How did you read that situation?

Sue Phillips: Well, when he was first approached, he and Greg Ervin, the deputy director at the time, did a lot of soul searching, a lot of talking, and a lot of thinking. The student from Cleveland was an interesting character, as I remember; and I didn't think the project had much of a chance at all of coming about.

It seemed like such an uphill battle to get the area he was talking about, the southeast Akron area, designated as a medically underserved area. And I thought that for a long, long time. But, I'll be darned; it came to fruition.

Interviewer: *Did you ever see Dr. Keck get mad?*

Sue Phillips: No. No, I never saw him lose his cool. He may have been upset at certain things that happened, but he would never lose control and take it out on anyone.

If there was an issue, he came to you; you sat down with him, you talked it out, and that was the end of it.

Interviewer: *You said you learned a lot from him. Can you give me an example?*

Sue Phillips: I learned so much from him. Being an assistant, you sometimes get pigeon holed, but he never wanted that for me.

If there was something I could do to help him, he trusted me to do it. I was able to visit the American Public Health Association in Washington, DC in 1991 when he was president of that organization, so that I could put faces with names and learn a little bit more about how the organization ran. Over the years, I had to learn to "collaborate" myself with the different organizations that he was involved in, and he allowed me to do that.

And I thought for an assistant, he really gave me an opportunity to get to know people and do some things on my own that maybe not everyone would have trusted their assistant to do.

I was involved in so many things that he was involved in. It gave me a greater appreciation of how hard he worked, and what it took to form collaborations on the local, state, national, and even international levels.

Working with him really broadened my horizons. I have the utmost respect for him. I always did and always will.

COLLABORATION CHECKLIST

The contributors to this book have given us the opportunity to learn a great deal about how each approaches opportunities for collaboration. I both enjoyed and learned from what they told us, and I hope you feel the same.

Collaborative partnerships are now an integral part of putting together the programs and services that are the key to improving the population's health status for public health practitioners or creating positive outcomes in many other societal and business ventures.

As our contributors have made clear, creating and managing collaborations is complex, but understanding the steps to collaborative success is quite straightforward. To aid in that understanding, we've teased out the major components in the first chapter and listed them for you below in summary fashion as a checklist for collaboration.

Our hope is that addressing these issues in a timely fashion will increase the likelihood that things will go well. If you're a novice, perhaps some of the mystery will disappear, and if you're experienced at this work, perhaps what we've prepared for you will provide some best practice hints that can help you over a hurdle or two.

A Checklist for Collaboration

- Prepare yourself to collaborate
  - Plan for the time and effort required
  - Develop personal relationships with your collaborative partners
  - Build mutual trust and respect
  - Practice humility – learn to put ego aside
  - Practice flexibility
  - Practice patience
  - Gain the support of your superiors and staff
  - Learn to be a "Systems Thinker"
  - Seek out mentors
  - Develop one or more trusted confidants
- Build the collaboration
  - Develop a clear shared vision
  - Choose the collaboration members
- Manage the collaboration
  - Define specific roles for each collaboration member
  - Set performance measures
  - Make the members into a "Learning Community"
  - Let go of the idea of ownership
  - Practice compromise
  - Share risks and rewards
  - Prepare to educate new members
  - Know when to leave a collaboration

- Other lessons learned
    - Keep your own agency or institution members informed
    - Turn losses into wins
    - Be prepared to go "Above and Beyond"

ARDITH KECK IMPRESSIONS

For me, the personal journey of working on this book with David and Bill was fun for many reasons.

As Bill's wife, I know him well and already have my own impressions of his character, but I admit I found it rewarding to think about all of our years together and all he's done in public health and in service to others. My "Duke of Hazard" (yes, he was given that title in Kentucky) has given of himself to people in so many ways.

I would say the book accomplishes the goals we had with the project from the onset: 1) To create a text which outlines the arc of actions which can culminate in successful collaborations of service to humanity; 2) To write a book which can help people reach their personal goals relating to collaboration; and 3) To craft a book which is fun to read and feels good to bring into your life.

I like the idea of "giving back," and I'm hoping this book does that very thing.

To me, each interview served a purpose, and I am appreciative of the contributions that reflect so much of life's wisdom.

As I look to the many years ahead for you, the reader, it is my sincere hope this book will be of service to you, encourage you to collaborate, and help you do so effectively, with the result that our world may be a bit brighter place for all.

Ardith

DAVID KETTLEWELL IMPRESSIONS

BILL KECK: A MAN WHO KNOWS SOME LESSONS THAT SHOULD BE PASSED ON

Bill, his wife Ardith, and I have struggled to create a book together. We had many meetings and conducted many interviews—each actually enjoyable.

As we approach the end of that road, Bill suggested I consider writing this section, and I am pleased to have an opportunity to do so.

First, let me give you a bit of history. I am not a public health expert, nor do I have any formal education in public health per se. I'm simply a writer and news journalist.

I was a news correspondent for a major news service, then executive author for the MGMA (Medical Group Management Association), producer of 230 TV shows and over 400 radio shows (most on public service topics including public health), and author of many books.

I met Bill when he invited me to see a film about the Cuban health system he served as a co-producer for called ¡Salud!

As I was producing TV shows that provided viewers with information on cancer, child abuse, elder abuse and mental illness, I felt I needed to understand the nation's health care needs in greater depth to cover Obamacare. So I asked Bill to be my mentor on all things medical, and he kindly accepted. I visited the medical school (now NEOMED), and we sat and talked.

My impressions of Bill were immediate—and have been long lasting.

I sensed his deep integrity, and the more I learned of his career, the more impressed I became.

When I saw his resume, I thought of Lincoln's statement that he'd consider granting commissions for military leadership by comparing letters of reference by the pound. It was endless—a compelling testament to a man who'd accomplished so very much in service to others in life.

I saw the quality of the man and sensed he knew things that should be passed on. That was the seed, the beginning.

And so I began to pester him, month-after-month, year-after-year, (I am a good pesterer using steady pressure like a drip of water) about doing a book that I saw as an homage of sorts, but more to the point perhaps as a blueprint for others to follow and emulate.

What reasonable person does not want to emulate excellence? Life is no fool's paradise.

The theme that took shape and resonated with Bill, his wife, and me, was a work on collaboration because we felt that was the root of the tree from which so many positive things in life come.

Collaboration: a paradigm that turns the work of one into the work of many, and due to the shared vision, creates a superorganism functioning at high levels.

As Dr. Yuval Noah Harari, Israeli Harvard scholar has said, it is mankind's ability to work in concert as one over great distances and time, which in large part explains our magnificent success as a species on this planet. [9]

I see collaboration as a tremendously powerful force, like electricity, latent perhaps in many cases but ready as potential energy to make a kinetic difference in any field of endeavor.

And I feel it's an underappreciated friend to us all—ready to awaken.

And so the project began.

Our collective thought was that collaboration might very well be a process, and more to the point, a repeatable process that can be explained and even taught at some level. Our expectations were not disappointed as this project developed.

When one approaches the study of piano, it is helpful to know what methods have brought good results for fine pianists worldwide in different times throughout musical history, and I believe this book does that to a greater or lesser degree for collaboration, thanks to Bill, Ardith, and all the exceptional contributors.

As we all get older, each of us asks what we've done that will survive us in life. I have no wife and no children, but I am a creative artist. My children are my writings and music, as I also play chromatic harmonica pretty well.

---

9   Harari, Yuval Noah. "Why Humans Run the World," YouTube video 17:08, filmed June 15, 20154, posted by TedTalk, July 24, 2015, http://www.youtube.cpom/watch?v=nzjWg4Dabs.

It is my hope that this book will survive and that it will make things better in some way.

At the very least, the book is a testimonial from people who know a good deal about collaboration, and a tribute to a great man and his wife, Bill and Ardith, and I have no qualms whatever about honoring those deserving of honor.

We live in a time of pernicious skepticism in government and are perceived as a fractured people. Organizational paradigms are under great stress here and abroad.

And yet, hope springs eternal—which it should.

In a world of skepticism, there is a place and a time to say something positive about wonderful people and wonderful happenings. This is that place, and this is that time.

I'm not much of a proponent of the "Life is Easy" or "Success Comes Easy" school. I see its premise as wholly false. So I must admit here that I don't see collaboration as easy. Not a bit. It's actually rather difficult.

So this book is crafted to help you down that path.

Am I idealistic? Certainly! I will not part with idealism.

IN CLOSING

As I look back on four decades of collaborative effort, I am struck by how much of the time I wasn't sure how things would work out. Doubt could be a nagging companion. The only recourse was to continue to move forward with clarity about the desired goal, managing issues as they arose. Resolving problems one by one adds to confidence and provides a real sense of progress.

I have had my share of failures, but as the narratives illustrate, sometimes work that did not achieve the original shared vision actually set the stage for success with an alternate goal, or created a base that others could use at a later date to move forward with the original intent. Much about the public health profession is about delayed gratification, and I feel good about contributing to alternate or delayed successes, even if I was not officially on the scene to enjoy them.

Human factors usually present the most serious challenges. Working with people you might not like so much at the beginning requires really listening to others' ideas and carefully and deeply considering them before speaking. It means mediating disputes and stroking strong egos, and sometimes it means accepting decisions you don't like in order to maintain progress. It means being slow to judge others while staying flexible—always staying flexible. It means being resilient in the face of problems and having the courage to deliver bad news when necessary.

Yes, it can feel like an emotional roller coaster much of the time, but if there are lows, there are also highs. I don't want to give the impression that the entire process was fraught with difficulties at all times. It was not. Actually, much of the time I spent working on collaborations was pleasant and rewarding, as it is likely to be for you.

I agree with Dr. Harari that our species' ability to work together to accomplish significant goals through creation of a shared vision is not only unique to us but is also essential if we are going solve the many problems that confront us on this earth.

You've noticed that each of these interviews contains a common root with some values shared by all; a basic understanding of how collaboration works. But it's equally true that each contributor defines collaboration in their own way which is individual and unique.

Each person's understanding reflects their own personality, talents, and inclinations. And of course, the environment in which they work.

Thus, there is a part of your understanding of collaboration which is shared by all, and a part that reflects you. Like a tree growing in the forest, unique.

That will make things more interesting, and points out the truism that collaboration is perhaps more an art than a science, or a bit of both.

I do want to again thank all those who contributed to this effort and let you know that Ardith and I wish you the very best in your personal collaborative efforts, and offer our universal "good luck" to all you may aspire to accomplish—working together.

Bill

BIBLIOGRAPHY

Franklin, Benjamin. *Poor Richard's Almanack.* New York: Peter Pauper Press, 1981.

Harari, Yuval N. *Sapiens: A Brief History of Humankind.* New York: HarperCollins, 2015. 31.

"Why Humans Run the World," YouTube video 17:08, filmed June 15, 2015, posted by TedTalk, July 24, 2015, http://www.youtube.cpom/watch?v=nzjWg4Dabs.

Hicks, Darrin K. and Carl E. Larsen. "Collaborating with Others." *Mastering Public Health: Essential Skills for Effective Practice.* Edited by Barry S. Levy and Joyce R. Gaufin. New York: Oxford University Press, Inc., 2012.

Leavitt, Mike and Rich McKeown. *Finding Allies, Building Alliances: 8 Elements that Bring-* and Keep- *People Together.* San Francisco, Jossey-Bass, 2013. PDF e-book.

Levy, Barry S. and Joyce R. Gaufin, ed. *Mastering Public Health: Essential Skills for Effective Practice.* New York: Oxford University Press, Inc., 2012.

Mattessich, Paul W., Marta Murray-Close, and Barbara R. Monsey. *Collaboration: What Makes it Work.* 2nd ed. St. Paul: Fieldstone Alliance, 2001.

Seng, Peter M. *The Fifth Discipline: The Art & Practice of the Learning Organization.* New York: Currency-Doubleday, 1990. Footnotes for Collaboration:

Made in the USA
Lexington, KY
28 April 2017